I0826855

If You Understood My Past You Would Understand My Praise

Darnyelle A. Jervey

If You Understood My Past, You Would Understand My Praise **is based on a true story. All characters are real people whose names have been changed and most events did occur.**

Incredible One Enterprises Publications, LLC
www.incredibleoneenterprises.com
560 Peoples Plaza #255 Newark, Delaware 19702

ISBN: 978-0-9820280-0-1
Library of Congress Control Number: 2008934741

Author photo by: Tonja C. Jennings
Book Cover by: Anointed Word Media Group

Printed in the United States of America

To order additional copies, please contact:
Incredible One Enterprises
1-888-801-5794
www.incredibleoneenterprises.com

In loving memory of my dear uncle

CURTIS EMMANUEL HENRY JERVEY
(1954 – 2008).

This book is dedicated to the memory of my uncle, Curtis E. Henry Jervey who departed this life unexpectedly while I was putting the finishing touches on this book. My Uncle Curt was one of my biggest supporters and he will be greatly missed. I do rejoice, however, because of God's soothing words "to be absent from the body means to be present with the Lord."

I love you Uncle Curt.

Here's what readers are saying:

"I thoroughly enjoyed the memoir written by brand new author Darnyelle Jervey, If You Understood My Past, You Would Understand My Praise. It takes courage to write about such personal issues, but knowing that they'd have an impact on someone else, she made it happen. In reading it, I laughed, cried, and also praised God for the many blessings in my life. I'm sure it has touched the lives of the many people who have read the book. I read her debut novel in two days and can't wait for the next book!" Thanks! T. *Matthews, Paralegal*

"I just finished reading your book "If You Understood My Past..." What a phenomenal read! I am an avid reader of anything inspirational and your book is right up there with the best. I usually don't expect much from a first novel, but yours was exceptionally well written and held my attention throughout. Bravo and kudos to you for endeavoring to share your story/testimony. Thank you for sharing your insight. It is a blessing to know that there are women, like myself, who consider developing and maintaining a relationship with the savior more important than sacrificing self for a "man." Be blessed, stay obedient and keep 'em coming! Ms. V. Jones, Administrator

"Ms. Jervey tells a humorous and vividly authentic narrative that many will find relatable and enjoyable. Her transparency will be embraced and undoubtedly lives will be changed. If You Understood My Past, You Would Understand My Praise will ignite an infectious belief in the victory that we all can achieve if we allow Jesus Christ to be the center of our joy; the true joy that world didn't give and the world can't take away!" M. Ann Ricks, author of Awesome Wonder: The Gift of Remembrance & The Son

"I couldn't put this book down. It kept me engaged page after page and I am so inspired by Ms. Jervey's authentic depiction of what a lot of women go through." S. Stephenson, author of Faith vs Fate

"I loved the book; it was outstanding. For a first time author, you hit it. I am already looking forward to the next one!" K. Booker, Accountant

"This book is for everyone, men and women. As a man, I too, learned about my praise and I am enjoying understanding the importance of self-love from a talented newcomer to the literary game." T. Wright, Business Owner

"I did just what Ms. Jervey said I would: I laughed, I cried, I prayed, I praised. No matter your station in life, you can learn from this book. Read and enjoy!" S. McNeil, First Lady

"I thoroughly enjoyed your book and now I can say that I understand your praise. Thank you for becoming transparent and sharing what I am sure was a tough life experience. I appreciate your humor and candor, you are a great writer. I wish you continued success." E. Gibson, Vice President

"Your authenticity is astounding. I have recommended this book to a lot of my teenage students so that they can be empowered NOW before your story becomes theirs. Thanks for enduring so that someone else might be blessed." S. Johnson, High School English teacher

"I read this book in three hours, I could not put it down. It kept me completely captivated and engaged and although I had not had the experiences shared on these pages, I could feel your past and praise. Great read." S. Thompson, Consultant

"Oh my goodness; what a gem! I was so inspired by your passion and influence through out your well written story. Thank you for sharing. This book is a must have." T. Dozier-Daniels, author of The Hidden Hand of God

"I so enjoyed this book. I felt empowered by your story. Thank you for sharing and I know that the next one is going to be out of this world." O. Ricketts, Entrepreneur

"The way that you were able to allow me to visualize each word on each page was amazing. What a gem. I am so inspired by you. You are on the verge of greatness." C. Harris, Marketing Executive

Acknowledgments

First and foremost, I give praise, honor and glory to God. Thank You for showing me that Your love is all I need. I thank You for the call You placed on my life to share bountifully with each reader of my story. God, I also want to thank You for giving me the courage to tell a story that I have buried inside of me for so long. Someone will be saved because of what You allowed me to experience for Your glory and I cannot thank You enough for this opportunity. I am so full of Your joy, as I bare all and become transparent for my readers. As I write, I feel the shackles coming off the feet of my readers. Let's dance!

To my parents, thank you for giving me life. I love you. Thank you for setting the ink on the page of my life. Thank you for believing in me and inspiring me to grow higher.

To my brothers and sisters, I love you. Thank you for stretching me.

To Nina Parker, you are my oldest and dearest friend. Thank you for the love we've known for one another since the beginning. I am so proud to call you my friend. Thank you for bestowing the honor of Godmother on me before I even knew of the God that would reside in me. Thank you for praying with and for me. Thank you for all your words of wisdom over the past six years and your friendship for the last thirty.

To Danine Huff, I may never be able to tell you how important your life has become to me. Thank you for allowing God to use you to open my eyes to the kind of love that I deserve. I can never thank you enough. You are priceless. Thank you for all that you did to aid my during this time, you are very appreciated.

To Antoine Oakley, you are a true friend until the end. I love you and I am so blessed to have had you as a constant in my life for twenty years. Thank you for being there when it all began with prayer, support and encouragement. Thank you for staying a true friend, who always wanted the best for me.

To Tonja Jennings, my personal photographer and friend and Veronica Wilkinson you have been my sound ear many a night and I am so glad that God saw fit to link our souls. I love and appreciate you. I never would have guessed how important you would become to me.

To Sharon Homer, you are so special to me. I thank you from the bottom of my heart for encouraging me, strengthening the iron that God made me and just for being a dear friend. I am so grateful that God made it so that you would become my assistant all those years ago and even after the job ended, you would remain my friend and confidante. I am praying for you.

To Melissa A. Ricks, my advanced reader and friend, thank you for your giving spirit. I appreciate you and all that you have done for me. I thank God for you. I thank God that He aligned us so that we can enjoy His perfect timing together.

To my church family, thank you for praying for me and helping me to truly get to know the lover of my soul.

Last but certainly not least, I would like to offer special thanks to all of the people along the way to developing my story. Good, bad or indifferent, each of you has shaped my experience and sharpened the iron that God made me. I am sure that at some point, we laughed, cried, argued, fought, prayed, danced and that has made all the difference. If you didn't get a special shout out, don't get upset. Charge it to my head and not my heart and know that you have been appreciated.

To the reader, thank you for giving my book a chance. It is my sincere prayer that your relationship with Christ is enhanced as you turn each page.

Preface

Therefore if any man be in Christ, he is a new creature: old things are past away; behold all things are become new.

2 Corinthians 5:17

As I looked back over my life and got caught up in praise, I realized that there was a story inside of me. I had something to say and I knew that people would listen to this insignificant girl who had dreams that were bigger than the hell in which she lived.

I am sharing shamelessly so that you may be enriched and blessed to start your own personal journey from *Past to Praise.*

My goal is simple: To help just one person realize that they are INCREDIBLE and as is such, they are entitled to much more than they are receiving and living right now.

I don't want any person to make the same mistake I made: putting confidence in man as opposed to trusting in the Lord.

I learned that everything that I ever wanted was on the other side of my fears. I will share those things that have helped to shape the woman that I am today. This journey is not void of struggle, bad mistakes, honest personal criticism, reflection or accomplishment. But I realized that in order to confirm my future, I had to conquer my past and that is what this book is all about. It is only a chapter in my story.

One thing I know for sure is that in order to appreciate me now, you have to get to know me then. We will cry together, dance together, sing together and laugh together.

I pray that you realize that if you seek first the Kingdom of God and His righteousness, as we are told in Matthew 6:33, you will be bountifully blessed and enriched. With God first, you will be entitled to a life of abundance.

Abundance is a mindset that once achieved will change everything! What I realized for sure is that life is all about Passion, Abundance, Confidence and Expectation. I learned that it was time to set an Incredible PACE in my life and the first step was journeying from my past to my praise.

Remember, if you can see the invisible, God can do the impossible, so dream the Incredible.

I pray that once you know my past, you'll understand my praise.

Please read, enjoy, cry, pray and be blessed.

Chapter 1

A fool's lips bring him strife, and his mouth invites a beating. A foul's mouth is his undoing, and his lips are a snare to his soul.

Proverbs 18: 6, 7

I remember like it was yesterday. I don't know if that is a good thing or a bad thing. But, I do. It happened on the fourth day of June; three days after my bridesmaids ordered their cranberry red two-piece *Bill Levkoff* halter-top dresses for our September wedding.

The dresses were beautiful. They were cranberry, a bold and powerful color, which was chosen specifically to illustrate the deep ties that we shared and were going to submit to on September 28th before God, our family and friends.

It was a Wednesday; the weather report said the day would be slightly overcast. And it was. The clouds in the sky were a grayish blue with a tint of gold. All day long, the sun had been playing peek-a-boo with the clouds. Wednesdays were always tough because I was only half way to solace in the weekend for personal time with family and friends. I had struggled immensely to get over the "hump" that week in particular and Friday couldn't come fast enough.

It happened three years and four months to the day that I met him and he changed my life forever. It has taken me years to realize what his entrance into my life would mean, and I do, I remember it like it was yesterday.

I had just gotten home from a laboriously challenging day at work. I had put my key into the front door, noticing that there was an unsightly dent in the bottom left hand corner. I am not sure why it stood out that day; I had been living in that house for three years and I had never noticed it once.

I shrugged it off with a "not now," as I crossed the threshold. I wasn't even in the house for a good ten minutes when the phone rang. I put my wedding planning book on the kitchen table and grabbed the phone on the third ring.

"Hello," I said, slightly annoyed. I assumed it was a telemarketer.

"We need to talk," he said.

I thought *what the devil?*

"Well, hello to you too."

"Some place public," he continued. His tenor voice was completely void of sentiment.

My heart sank. Instantly I knew something was wrong.

Why meet in public? What is going on? I thought.

"Okay. What happened? Is something wrong, somebody hurt?" I immediately assumed the worse.

"No, everyone is fine. I just want to talk."

He attempted to soothe me with his "calm" voice. Suddenly his voice became extra syrupy, complete with a little song at the end of every other word.

It didn't work. I was bracing myself for a big blow.

"Where? Why? What's going on?" I became agitated, my voice started to rise and I needed answers. I did not like surprises. I always needed to know what I was getting myself into.

"We need to talk in person, not over the phone. Meet me at the Riverfront Park at five-thirty." The line went dead.

I stood lingering; I stared at the phone for another minute or two.

"Okay, I said," with a lot of attitude. I was thoroughly exasperated. I rolled my eyes, sucked my teeth, and took a deep breath as I put the cordless phone back on the charger. I immediately started concocting scenarios in my mind.

I already knew what this was about. I had known for at least three months but I didn't want to believe it. I would have to put my plans for some classical music while I made dinner on hold for now.

I grabbed my purse and headed right back out the door.

"Sorry, Chopin," I yelled as the front door closed and locked behind me.

As I drove downtown, my mind raced. I jumped onto I-95 north thinking about what had just happened. What was he going to say?

We'd been distant for months, during our entire engagement, actually. Whoever said that your engagement is the happiest time of your life is a bold-faced liar! At least they were a liar when speaking about Trenton and me.

Since I am telling the truth, I had been miserable ever since I said, "yes, I will." It really started a long time before I agreed to his request for my hand in the K-Mart parking lot where we met; but we swept our issues under the rug and pretended like everything was okay. But everything was wrong and had been for quite some time.

I remember that the Sounds of Blackness hit *Be Optimistic* was on the radio and I laughed. I couldn't be optimistic but I thought it was ironic that the radio was playing that song at the exact moment that I needed optimism. I was kind of anxious and extremely nervous. I was going over it again and again in my head to no relief.

What would he say? How would I respond? Was I ready for this conversation? Ready or not, it was about to hit the fan.

Deciding that jumping to conclusions was probably not the best thing to do since I was already on edge; I tried to calm myself down by putting the radio on the gospel station, WDAS AM. A fast song was playing and I couldn't really get into it, so I turned the radio off all together.

As I drove the remaining ten minutes, I decided to tune into God's frequency.

"Lord, as always, first I just want to thank You because of who You are. I know we don't talk as much as we should and I know that I like to do things my way, but today, I need You in the worst way. I have no idea what I am walking into. I am coming to You now to ask for some strength and wisdom. Please keep me calm and focused. I pray this prayer in Jesus' name, amen."

My sanity was unraveling, but talking to God eased the angst building in my chest. As I tried to breathe slowly and methodically, I cringed at the thought of what was waiting for me when Trenton and I were face to face.

The thought of meeting Trenton in public to "talk" really had me on edge. There was just something about having to talk about issues that always made me a little apprehensive, regardless of the person with whom I was going to have the conversation. I am a worrywart and I always assumed the worse. I believed that I was always the problem. I could convince myself at any given moment that if we needed to talk, it was about me and why I was no longer what the person I was talking to was looking for.

I drove the rest of the way to the park in silence concentrating on my drive and allowing God's peace to penetrate me; I was freaking out and needed to calm myself down. It was a good thing that I had skin, because I felt like I was going everywhere at once. I had been dreading this conversation for three months by acting like I saw and heard no evil. I had a habit of holding things in and then erupting like a volcano. I could feel my lava starting to rise. Trenton had been getting on my last nerve but I allowed myself to be stressed and bothered without letting him know for fear that he would leave me.

I had a deep-seated issue: I feared being alone. My biggest fear was that no one would want me or love me when it was all said and done. I convinced myself that if I spoke my mind, I would chase people away. And I wasn't ready for Trenton to go.

I had a desire to call on God again but resisted it. Sometimes, I did not feel comfortable monopolizing His time when I didn't treat Him like He deserved. I talked to God like I took my ibuprofen, as needed.

I definitely took a lot of creative liberties when it came to the Word of God and somehow, right now, I didn't want to push my luck because I really needed Him to show up and show out on my behalf when I got to the Riverfront.

I went to church as a child but it was a dull and boring place. When I wasn't dozing off, I did learn enough to know that if you called on Him, He would be there. I was so glad He was. I was elated that He hadn't been so quick to abandon me like I had often abandoned Him. I had developed a spirit of apostasy; yet, I was pleased that He was best known for His grace and mercy. I was relieved that He never dropped me like a bad habit because I needed Him now like nobody's business.

I was glad for that sea of forgetfulness. Lord knows that I had more than a few sins floating in the sea.

There wasn't a lot of traffic that Wednesday so I got to the MLK Blvd exit in no time flat. Off the ramp, down the street, two right turns, and I arrived at the park. I found a parking spot quickly, looked around, and didn't see Trenton, so I waited.

Starting to lose my newly gained cool I checked my car clock, it was 5:20 pm; I was a little early.

That day, I thought those extra ten minutes would kill me. I was never good with surprises. Like Janet Jackson, I had to be in control. But I had no choice. Trenton had me in a barren wasteland waiting to be rescued. And so I waited.

Out of the corner of my eye, I saw a couple smiling intently at one another as they walked hand in hand and I cringed. I wanted that so bad. Even though I had a fiancé, I never knew the joy in their eyes. The warmth of their smiles was foreign to me. I felt that it was amazing that I never knew the kind of love that moved me to tears like I watched on a television screen. And I knew that it was possible because I had watched many of my friends experience a love like I craved like a *Snickers* bar.

It always struck me as weird that the thought of spending the rest of my life with Trenton didn't make me weak at the knees. I didn't even cry when he proposed. I always felt so much intensity when I watched couples on television and it seemed like robbery that I couldn't recreate the same feelings with my real live fiancé. That should have been my first clue.

I checked my watch again; it was 5:23 p.m. I shut my eyes, took a slow, melodic yet deep breath and it seemed as if that as soon as I did, I was startled by a knock on my passenger car door window. I jumped to see Trenton's smiling face. Somehow, however, I couldn't smile back.

I took another deep breath and let him in.

"Hey," he said as he got into the car. He leaned in to kiss my cheek. Robotically, I leaned in too. His lips felt bitter and arid. The skin on them scratched me a little as he grazed my cheek. I looked over at him; he was definitely shaken and yet I knew that he was about to rock my world and change everything. I could clearly see the angst in his left cheek.

"Hey." I replied in a profuse tone. I wasn't in the mood for games or pretending that I was as cool as a cucumber. I was coming apart at the seams.

"So, how was traffic?" Trenton asked.

I peered at him. Was he for real? He was not trying to make small talk, was he? Well, I nipped that in the bud real quick.

"What's up?" I said, complete with a little neck cranking action. I never wanted to beat around the bush; I was definitely a straight shooter.

He took a deep breath. "How was your day?"

"My day was okay. Look, Trenton. You wanted to talk and in *public* no less, so let's talk, what's up?"

I had no time for small talk. I felt like screaming "Get to it, already!"

"Okay, okay." He took a deep breath. It felt like five minutes went by while he was breathing intensely. I presumed he was trying to calm himself down because I knew good and well that he knew better than to lash out at me.

"I wanted to talk with you today because what I have to say affects our future." He sighed, this time even more deeply than before.

"Okay?" I prodded. I rolled my eyes in his direction.

Here it comes, I thought.

"Okay, here it is," he mumbled under his breath loud enough for me to hear, as if he could suddenly read my clouded mind. He looked away from me and cleared his throat. "I lied when I told you I never slept with her." He turned a little more in the opposite direction.

I cringed as he said the words I knew yet dreaded to hear.

His body language depicted that he really wished he were telling me this over the phone. He couldn't even say her name but I knew exactly to whom he was referring.

She was old enough to be his mother. Twenty years his senior, *she* was a 45-year-old woman from Trenton's church that I had joined about six months ago, so I guess it was really *our* church. They were trustees together. She had been gunning for Trenton ever since I could remember and probably even before that.

As soon as I joined, I could tell there was something about her that I didn't like. You know how you can just tell? Something about someone just doesn't sit well with you? Well, she didn't stand well with me either. As they say, 'trust your gut.' My gut told me that she was up to no good.

I remember the very first time that she crossed my peripheral vision. Even before I knew that she was a friend of Trenton's, I could already sense that she was not to be trusted. Maybe you should call it woman's intuition.

She taught my new members class. She was always trying to find reasons to ask questions about Trenton and I since, at that time, I was the only new member in the class. And since I wasn't stupid, I never fed into her probes for information. It was none of her business.

There was just something pretentious about her. She was too clingy, hanging on every single man in the congregation. She was always talking so loud to make sure that everyone could hear how important she wanted you to think she was.

You know that one person who had a response for every word the Pastor preached? You know that obnoxious voice that stifles your praise? You roll your eyes and try to focus?

"You better preach." "Tell him Pastor." "Thank you Lord, thank you for Pastor." "Come on now, they're not ready for this Word." "It's tight but it's right church." "Y'all better fall in line with the Word."

She was the one who said "Amen" louder than everyone else. She stood up every time the choir got up to sing. She treated the church's center aisle like it was her personal runway as she paraded in skirts with hems that stopped well before the level deemed appropriate for church. She always wiggled just a little too much from her front pew in her form fitting dresses, on any given Sunday. The one who gave every man a hug after church was over, that was Constance.

When praise is genuine, it is the best thing in the world. When it's not, it just looks foolish. Constance looked absurd. She was as transparent as Scotch tape. I could see right through her and her intentions. I didn't even know her last name. But I did know that she cooed like a baby whenever Trenton was around and it made me sick to my stomach.

On numerous occasions, I confronted him about the way she hung on his every word. He always denied the impact of her "friendliness."

"You know she wants you right?"

"Who? Constance? No, it's not like that. She's like a big sister."

"Well, if that is the case, she is into incest because she doesn't want you to be a brother."

"Why don't you give her a chance? She really is a nice person."

"I don't want to give her chance. When I am around her, something in my spirit doesn't feel right. I can't ignore that." Who did he think he was trying to tell me how to feel about her? I knew she wasn't worthy of a chance.

"I think that if the two of you ever talked, you'd think differently."

As I recalled one of those many conversations in my mind, I got pissed.

I glanced over at him; he was looking so pitiful. I could tell that he was extremely uncomfortable. It served him right. After what he had put me through, he deserved to be feeling some kind of way. I wanted to make it worse.

"She's pregnant, isn't she?" I asked. Actually, it was more of a statement than a question. I already knew the answer.

In my mind, that was the only reason why we were having this "public" conversation. If she weren't, he would not fess up and take the chance that we would not get married in three months. He knew that with us all attending the same church and her belly growing, someone would put two and two together. If they hadn't already.

I was no fool, he probably wanted some applause for telling me himself but his telling me was his way of covering his behind and attempting to save face.

Trenton knew I was his meal ticket. He had a failing business but I was an up and coming superstar at the firm. I was getting promoted left and right. And silly me, I would give him money and pay his bills when he had a short month.

I had always been so loyal. Although that is a good thing, I was always taken advantage of. I always said yes, gave my all and always got dogged out and not just by men, sometimes my so called friends and family would get me too.

I could tell that I was being defecated on again.

When would I learn?

He turned away again. I could hear him breathing intently. Since I didn't get an immediate response, I assumed he didn't hear me. I repeated myself, this time not nearly as nice.

"Didn't you hear me ask you a question?" I turned to face him head on and with a voice filled with contempt and growing anger.

Again, he sighed deeply. He was wearing me out.

"Answer me!" I screamed at him.

I was really about to lose it. He was sitting there all discombobulated like someone had stolen his bike. He created this monster and now he was taking his sweet time continuing his confession. I had had enough.

In the nick of time, he bowed his head and cut his eyes up at me before he responded, "Yeah."

Chapter 2

The man who says, "I know him" but does not do what he commands is a liar, and the truth is not in him.

I John 2:4

I was a little stunned by his admission to what I knew had to be the case. Even though I knew the truth, it took me by surprise. My mind was trying desperately to process the fact that we were twenty-five years old and he had gotten seduced by a woman old enough to be his mother. And what's more, he had gotten her pregnant. I felt sick. I was enraged.

Hearing him answer positively to my question took a lot out of me. But somehow I mustered up the strength, balled up my fist and packed a punch so powerful that his head hit the car window with a loud thump. It surprised him; it definitely surprised me!

I didn't say anything at first; I just cut him deep with my espresso brown eyes. My look was so intense; I bruised his heart. If looks could kill, I would be writing this book on death row.

He tried to get out of the car. It was actually kind of funny to watch his stunned demeanor, as a result of my sucker punch. He fumbled desperately trying to get a good grip on the car door handle.

In a loud, commanding voice, I said "You better stay right where you are. You coward. If you had the balls to sleep with her, if you had the balls to come here and tell me this three months before our wedding; then have the balls to follow it through."

My fist was balled up ready to hit him again. I must admit, it felt really good to hit him. It felt really good to command his attention. It was definitely empowering. In that one punch, I felt like a novice boxer after winning his first bout by knockout. I felt like I had not been a sucker for three years.

Part of the reason I was still with Trenton was because I felt he owed me something, after all he'd put me through, I was waiting on my prize.

As I sat there with my fist tingling from impacting his dark face, I felt that I was getting closer to claiming that prize. Albeit different, this feeling was a prize nonetheless.

With that punch, I felt like I had confidence in my worth and myself. I was mad as hell for allowing him to have his way with my emotions and it was over. Over.

I felt like I was taking back some of the power I had given to him during our relationship. I was, indeed, focused on taking back what he stole from me.

One tear cascaded down my caramel colored cheek. I shook my head trying to resist the urge to cry.

I will not cry, I told myself. *Get it together and be strong*, I screamed in my head. *You will not let him see you cry.*

I was always so loyal. I was a fool. I always gave all of me to the man that was in my life. I typically allowed myself to get lost in his sauce. I consistently focused my eyes on the thought of finally being loved like I had longed for all my life and each time, I was let down and once again, I had nothing.

Right then, sitting across from the man that was supposed to be my husband, I felt like the character Angela Bassett portrayed in *Waiting to Exhale* when her husband told her as she was getting ready to go out to the dinner party that he was taking the other woman instead of her because she, the other woman, did not want to be alone that night. Man. You know when Mary J. sang *I'm Not Gone Cry*. I could hear the music being cued up in my head as this scene in my real life drama started. As Mary belted out the lyrics to the song, I thought about being his lover and a secretary. I put in a lot of work, 7 days a week and I was always doing my part, helping him get up and running. You know the song. And yes, that was me. But I do thank God that it hadn't been eleven years of sacrifice. As it turned out, three years was more than enough.

Seeing the best in people and wanting to believe in others at all costs was an expensive character trait. It had cost me more than money on several occasions, and in the last three years, it had cost me everything.

"I was hoping that this wouldn't matter." He turned to face me. He smiled with his eyes, searching mine for understanding and forgiveness. He was serious.

I laughed on the inside. He was a fool to think that I would be okay with all of this.

"I still want to marry you. She means nothing. She caught me at a weak moment, that's all. I don't love her, I love you." He spouted, like he had rehearsed his lines a thousand times.

I couldn't resist the urge to convey the sentiments from the line Halle Berry made famous in *Boomerang*. "Love should've kept you loyal to me and us and what we were building together." I went on to say, "I gave you everything and all you did was take it." I looked at his pitiful soul cowering in the seat beside me.

I was livid; actually, pissed is a better word for how I felt. I was mad as hell. And when a woman's fed up…

I didn't even realize it when I heard another thump against the car window. I had hit him again. This time my fist took on a life of its own and punished him with a piece of the pain that was slowly but surely filling my heart.

He peered at me, this time stunned and wounded, but he didn't try to get out of the car. He raised his voice an octave higher than I had ever heard him speak.

"It meant nothing. I promise. I realize now more than ever how much I love you. You are everything to me. I want a future with you."

"You realize now? What have you been realizing for the past three years?"

"I made a mistake but I know that it's you I want."

"And what happens when she spreads her legs again?"

"It won't happen again. I promise."

"Your word is not accepted here."

"I mean it, she meant nothing."

"So it was just this one time, then? And coincidentally, she got pregnant?"

Just for kicks, I asked him that. I already knew the answer.

What's more, it didn't matter; my mind was made up. It was over. After all of the late nights that had been unaccounted for, I still needed this as a reason to finally walk away. When I think back to all the times I called and didn't get an answer or got out of my bed in Bear and drove the twenty minutes to Wilmington and sat in his living room waiting for hours and he never came home or came in late, I hung my head in shame. I always fell for his "I'm working late" lies because I couldn't bring myself to believe that he wouldn't keep the promise he made to me that he would never hurt me. It hurt like hell.

"Well, no. It's been going on for about six months. Once we got engaged, I really started to second-guess myself and my confidence plummeted. She was there for me…"

Did he really just say that? Maybe I was dreaming.

"Of course she was." I cut him off, pissed that he had the nerve to fix his lips and say that she was there for him. I, too, had been there.

What about all the times I was there for him? I pondered inwardly.

"You and that depression stuff. 'Because life was not going your way' was crap. I told you that the only one who could change your situation was you. You know that I was not going to write, direct and co-star in your pity parties. We had been there, done that and gotten the t-shirt. I have way too many T-shirts with you Trenton." I was looking him dead in his face.

"I know you have been patient with me that is what I love about you. You have never given up on me."

I ignored his comment and instead continued on my path of rage. "So let me guess, first she stroked your ego, and then she told you that you were a great guy and I didn't understand you…."

"That's not how it happened." He cut me off abruptly. I could see his veins pulsing and his blood boiling. I could tell that he felt a piece of the rage burning in my heart.

"Well, you know what, save it. I don't even want to know how it happened; the only thing that matters to me is that it did. And I do not want a man who cheats on me after he asks me to be his wife. And to top it all off, you had the nerve to have gotten her pregnant? You had that much respect for me that you had consistent unprotected sex with her? That is low Trenton, even for you. Of all the things you could tell me right now, the fact that you got her pregnant is blowing my mind. I cannot believe you."

I turned away trying to prevent that pesky tear from falling into my lap. I was clear; he would not see me cry.

"Please talk to me. We can work this out." He grabbed my hand and I abruptly snatched it back.

I laughed as I turned back to face him. "Thanks for showing me how much you love me. I am so full of rage that I cannot stand the sight of you." I turned away and gingerly wiped a tear from my deep-set eyes. *I will not let him see me cry. Get it together, girl. You will not cry,* I told myself.

"Well, we haven't been together in months. You wouldn't let me touch you. I have my needs." He had the nerve to have a smug look on his face, like that was his validation!

"I know that I did not just hear you say what I think I heard you say." I was heated, and my neck was moving back and forth vigorously.

I felt like Tina in *What's Love Got to Do With It* when she was in the limo finally standing up to Ike. I wanted to punch him a third time. I wanted to beat the three years that I spent in fear of living without him all the way out of him.

"You know why we weren't physically intimate anymore. You said you understood. We said we were going to wait so that our wedding night would be special." I looked at him and rolled my eyes. "Well, I waited."

Why hadn't I just cut my losses and gone almost three years ago?

"Look," his voice rising, "why it happened no longer matters, what does matter is that I made a mistake. I cheated on you. There, I said it. God has forgiven me, why can't you?" He rationalized.

"No you didn't just pull the God card on me. You conveniently want God to be a part of our relationship *now*? After all the dirt you've done? You, a trustee and being groomed for deacon, sleeping with a fellow trustee and *now*, you want me to have God's heart of forgiveness? Puh-lease. Where were God and His way of escape when you were having your cake and eating it too? I can't forgive you right now. It isn't that easy for me. God is known for His grace and mercy, not me. I am sure one day I may, but that day is not today. I mean seriously, do you really think that you are going to have it your way? I am not Burger King"

"Baby, I love you. I can't change the fact that she is pregnant and I have to handle my responsibility but I love you and I want you to be my wife."

"People in hell want ice water; how does it feel to want? You should have thought about that before you cheated on me." I scolded him.

He turned away and put his head down. He sniffled. He was crying. *What a punk.*

"I'm so sorry," he said in between teary gasps for breath. "After all we've been through, I deserve another chance." He pleaded.

"*Because* of all we've been through, you don't."

"It shouldn't matter that I messed up."

I scoffed at him, "It does matter. You *really* do think you can have your cake and eat it too? Well, you can starve for all I care. You chose her and yes, you have to handle your responsibility but I'll remove one thing from your plate: me. I am no longer among the things that should concern you."

I reached over to open his door from the inside but stopped short suddenly. "Wait a minute. Are you even sure it's your baby? I am sure that you are not the only man who belonged to someone else that she is creeping with." I am not really sure why I cared enough to ask him that.

"Well, it is too soon for a paternity test but we have been together frequently for months."

"And I bet that most of the times have been unprotected, right?" His words had managed to throw me another slap in the face. I flinched internally. I could feel my face burning with anger.

"At first we were careful, but soon it became so much of a hassle."

I couldn't believe this fool. He went from lying to baring his soul and it was wearing me out.

"So you wanted something like this to happen?"

I am going to have to call my doctor to schedule a full set of tests for sexually transmitted diseases. I had no idea where that woman has been, I thought to myself.

"No, I never expected her to get pregnant, she *is* 45." He bowed his head. I think he realized how stupid he sounded after the words were released from his mouth.

"You are more stupid than I thought. You know that women are having babies into their 50's."

"She told me that she couldn't have children, which was why at her age she was still childless."

"And of course your naïve behind believed her. It was more likely that no man was fool enough to sleep with her without protection. That should've told you something." I couldn't believe how stupid he sounded.

"I didn't see any reason for her to lie to me." He actually sounded as if he believed that statement.

"So the fact that she knew you had a fiancée and came onto you, didn't lead you to believe that she shouldn't be trusted? Wow." I was so astonished by his lack of intelligence.

"I guess I wasn't thinking." He lowered his voice and bowed his head. As his head shook back and forth, I felt a little temporary relief from my own pain. He was a fool.

"I think that is the truest thing you have said since you got into my car. No, Trenton, you weren't thinking and you still aren't. If you think for one second that I would marry you after you betrayed me, you are a fool. I don't trust you and I would never be in a relationship, let alone a marriage, where I had to keep you under lock and key just to know you were not cheating on me. You know what they say, 'once a cheater, always a cheater.' I would never again put my trust in you. That's word and you can take that check to the bank and cash it." As I said it, I believed it as sure as I knew my name.

"Don't say that. I know that we can work this out. Let's just meet with Pastor Jenkins. I know that if we go to counseling we can fix this."

Again, I laughed. "You want to go to counseling? We just got out of counseling. You can't keep your hands to yourself after you asked me to marry you, while we were in premarital *counseling* and you think that going to more counseling with your Pastor, who by the way, probably knew about your little tryst all along, will be able to help salvage our relationship? No, you can't think that I am stupid enough to fall for that." I shook my head in disbelief of his ignorance.

Had I really appeared that gullible all these years?

All of a sudden, it was crystal clear. I could see clearly now the love dust was gone. It was like the Red Sea was in front of me and Trenton was behind me. I knew I needed to head towards the Promise Land without him. I was leaving him in the wilderness. Love didn't live here anymore.

Trenton was black history, but he wouldn't even be celebrated in February.

"No, we can't fix this." I continued. "At least we cannot in a way that will make you happy." I was finally comfortable with the fact that he was no longer the man for me. He never was. I had tried and tried for years to make him the right man when he had proved long ago that he wasn't man enough for the job.

"But I promise," he sighed and raised his voice to make his point. "She doesn't mean anything to me."

"I'm sure that she doesn't see it that way," I countered sarcastically.

What a fool. Men are a trip, they think they can do their dirt yet when they get caught people won't react adversely to them? How dumb is that?

"I don't care what she thinks. I want a future with you. You are the one I want to spend the rest of my life with; how can I get you to see that?"

"First of all, you can't. For the first time in a long time it is my clear sight that is preventing me from wavering in any way. Second of all, wow, you are almost convincing. Did you practice that over and over? Did she help you run your lines to make it sound sincere?"

I paused to let my callous words sink in. "It is over. Get out of my car. I will be in touch for you to get your things from my place and I will give you a chance to get together the money you owe me for the wedding as well as the loan."

"For the wedding? What money? I thought you handled all of the wedding stuff." Trenton looked at me with confusion in his soul.

"I know you don't think that you are getting off easy. All the non-refundable deposits have been made and the way I see it, the reason we are not getting married is because of your indiscretions so I want my money back. I paid the DuPont Country Club, the photographer, the DJ and the florist. And all of them are non-refundable. Not to mention the $1800 loan I gave you to pay your bills last month. Look, get out. I will contact you when I am ready to settle up. I encourage you to not allow your fingers to dial my number."

Chapter 3

In times of disaster they will not wither; in days of famine they will enjoy plenty.

Psalm 37:19

After he got out of the car, I sped off. I didn't even know what to do or where to go. Although I knew that I didn't want him anymore in my head, my heart was keeping an altogether different timetable.

I said the first thing that popped into my head out loud over and over. "*God grant me the serenity to accept the things I cannot change, the courage to change the things I can; and the wisdom to know the difference.*"

I just kept saying it out loud over and over. It gave me some peace. But, I was pissed. I wanted to fight. I wanted to punch him again. No, I wanted to whip his behind.

I wanted to beat him like he had stolen something. Truthfully, he had. He had taken my pride, my self-esteem, my confidence and my self-worth. And what's more was the fact that I had given it to him, of my own free will. He had stolen three years of my life that I would never get back.

I had so much anger pent up inside of me and I didn't know how to get rid of it. The prayer helped; but let me keep it real; I was still pissed. I wanted to hit some thing; or better yet, someone.

Constance, I wanted to beat her down for sure. I knew where she lived. I could go over there and whip her behind.

You will do no such thing.

I wanted to scream. I pulled my car over, rolled down all the windows in my sand colored Mazda whom I had affectionately named "Sandy" and screamed.

"Aaaaaaaaaaaaaaaaaaaaaaaaah," I let out a deep scream from the pit of my stomach. I started to shake because I screamed so loud. I felt it deep down in my soul. It got caught in the back of my throat a few times. I know it was all of the frustration I had felt for months; no years, trying to break lose. I let it go. I think I screamed for a few minutes straight without a breath. It felt so good.

We were through. It was over and I was okay with it. There would be no reconsiderations. There would be no relenting and changing my mind or giving him one more chance. After what he had cost me over the years, he was a done deal.

When I finally came up for air, I cried. Man, I cried. I cried out to the Lord. I cried to myself. I cried in pity. I cried out in embarrassment. I was a weak, vulnerable mess. God was the only one that could help me.

I knew the Lord. Unfortunately, at that time in my life, we knew each other real well on Sunday but Monday through Saturday, we didn't hang out. Our relationship had been strained for a long time. I had kept him on the back burner until I needed him for years. We were on and off again lovers, and even then Jesus and I had one-day stands.

I loved Him when I needed Him to get me out of something. You know those, "Lord, if you just get me out of this one" moments with God? That was typically how our conversations started. I wanted to live believing that as long as I went to church on Sunday and paid my tithes, everything would be all right.

I kept crying incessantly. One of my problems was that when I cried, snot came from every orifice on my face and got everywhere. Snot was on the steering wheel, in my hair, on my seat, on the driver's side door, on the passenger's side door, on the window, on the console, all over my face, it was everywhere. To top matters off, it started to drizzle, then the sky collapsed and it rained vigorously. It was coming down in buckets.

I took a deep breath and howled. "Lord, what else can go wrong today?" I didn't know how much more I could take.

My phone rang. It was a number I didn't recognize so I pulled myself together quickly and answered. I wasn't yet ready to put my business in the street so I had to pretend like all was well.

"Hello," I disguised my pain. I did my best to sound like normal.

"Are you satisfied now?" an unrecognizable female voice sneered at me.

"Who is this?"

"You know who this is. I've got your man and his child now, how does it feel?" She was smiling.

"Trick, I know you did not just dial my phone number with this mess. Like I told him, you can have him but let me give you a tip. He ain't worth it. He will cause more pain than good, but go ahead, if you think you are the best woman for the job, handle it. You are a pitiful soul to have to get your validation by preying on other people. I hope you rot."

I started to hang up but then I decided to add one more thing. "And, know that if you ever fix your fingers to dial my number again, I will come to your home and beat you like you stole something. I will put something on your behind that soap and water cannot wash off. Try me if you want, but I advise you to forget my phone number."

I hung up the phone. I was fuming. I couldn't believe that she had the audacity to call me. Who in the world did she think she was? How did she get my number? Didn't she know that she was just sloppy seconds?

I fumed for a little bit longer and then I broke down and cried, again. I was so lost and I didn't want to be alone so I picked up the phone. I sped through my speed dials and just as I was about to dial out, Trenton's mother's cell phone number crossed the screen.

"Hello." I said letting the pain sear through my vocal chords.

Mrs. Peterson immediately sensed my pain. "Hey there," she paused. "How are you sweetie?" She sounded extremely concerned.

"Not so good. Have you talked to Trenton?" I couldn't believe that I cared.

"Yes, he just called. I am so sorry. I pray that the two of you can work it out. He really does love you. He was just being a man." She was defending her son; of course that was to be expected.

Why did women always pass off what men did as 'he's just being a man?' Why couldn't we set higher standards of ethics with our sons to prevent them from thinking that 'being a man' gave them the right to disrespect women?

"No, we can't. I don't want to." I stammered between the tears.

"Baby, don't throw away all that you have meant to one another over this. I'll tell you that something similar happened to me with Trenton, Sr. when we were dating and preparing for marriage. I stayed with him and it has made our relationship much stronger. Give Trenton a chance, he really does love you."

Again, I found myself thinking back to Tina Turner, *What's love got to do with it*? I asked myself.

"No disrespect, Mrs. Peterson, but I am not you. I do not believe in entering into a marriage with deceit at the forefront and I can never excuse the fact that he got her pregnant. He got her pregnant. That still baffles me. If a relationship is not based on trust, it can never survive. I just can't do that. I won't do that; maybe I haven't always held myself in high enough regard but at this point, I know that I am worth more. I did everything for him. I was always there through all of the stuff he did to me. I stood by his side. If he loved me, then he would have stayed true to us."

I took a deep breath and blew my nose as I was starting to sound very congested.

"I know baby. But give it time. I know things will work themselves out."

She wasn't hearing me. "I mean we just graduated from our premarital counseling in April. So while we were learning how to be husband and wife, he was already excelling at being an adulterer. I can't pretend that I don't have that information. I finally value myself more than to allow Trenton to continue to use me as his doormat. He will always think it is okay to step out on me, if I let him get away with this."

Why are you explaining your decision to her? A still small voice asked me.

"Listen, I am not even sure why I answered the call; this was a mistake. Goodbye."

I abruptly hung up the phone. Then I turned my cell phone off. Enough was enough.

Why had I answered her call? I asked myself as I grabbed another tissue and continued to clear my sinuses.

I couldn't shake the brewing contempt in my heart. It was filling up the space rapidly and removing all rational thought. For two seconds, I considered going to his house.

I wanted to hit him again. I wanted to make him understand what his indiscretion had done to me; it was killing me softly, yet I wasn't ready to die.

It was still raining and I was so tired and weak, too weak to move. I just let the rain beat down on Sandy and sat there perplexed.

Maybe I was dreaming. Maybe any minute I would realize that I was on *Candid Camera*. Or, maybe Ashton was on his way over to reveal that I had been punk'd.

I still felt like I needed someone to talk to but I couldn't call any of my friends, I was too embarrassed. What would they say? How would they act? I felt so alone.

I had always put up such a front like I had it going on when really I was so low and felt so badly about myself. Deep down, where no one could see, I was jacked up.

I felt sure that I was not the first woman to call off her wedding but right now, I felt like an island.

My heart was heavy so I turned to the only place I could. I turned to the Lord.

I began to pray out loud, "Lord, please lead me to a place in Your Word that will comfort me during this time. I don't know what else to do, God. I know that I am not perfect; but I do know that I can call on You and You will deliver me. Please, dear Lord, deliver me from the despair that I feel at this time. Please let Your Word minister to me and guide me as to what I need to do to pick up the pieces of my broken existence. I pray this prayer in Jesus' name, amen.

Then, right there pulled over in the Comcast parking lot on Route 13, I opened my Bible and somehow I knew to turn to Psalm 32:10, which read *many sorrows shall be to the wicked; but he who trusts in the Lord, mercy shall surround him.* The scripture comforted me slightly. I needed mercy to surround me. I was so broken.

As I read that passage, I felt like someone had removed a heavy weight from my shoulders. I felt like God himself was saying "give it to me, I'll hold onto the pain for you. Just trust me, give your heart to me."

Like someone had just flipped the switch on in my life, I knew the answer. That was it; the only way I could move on was to trust the Lord. I couldn't trust Trenton, I couldn't trust myself, and at that moment I couldn't even trust my friends. But I could trust God. I could reach out to Him. I knew that somewhere in the Word it said that if I cast my cares on Him, my burdens would be lightened. Right then and there, I made a decision that I was going to be okay and that I was going to allow God to guide me. How He would guide me and what would happen, I didn't know; but I was at a point when I was willing to trust Him completely.

The more I thought about it, I realized that this happened because God had allowed it. I remembered the story of Job and that the devil had to get God's permission to attempt to destroy Job's life. I knew for certain that even then, He dispatched His angels all around me to protect me from what would have become of me if I stayed with Trenton. I knew the Bible told me that He would never give me more than I could bear and I knew I could not bear anymore of my existence being swallowed by Trenton. Trenton had become a taker and he took everything about me that wasn't nailed down. Unfortunately, that was everything that mattered.

The rain started to let up enough for me to see my way home. It took me another forty minutes because I had an emotional breakdown at every light along the way. Each cry break weakened me and I couldn't wait to get home.

As I pulled up to my house and parked in my driveway, I started to cry again. I just couldn't believe that I had started this day with a good sense of my future. I was excited that the wedding plans were really coming together. I was going through my checklist, getting things accomplished. I had just confirmed a few more appointments and scheduled a few more vendor visits. And with the bridesmaids' dresses ordered, that was huge burden lifted. We had just finished our Bridesmaids weekend and I was scheduled to meet with the florist the next day to finalize the flowers.

I looked down at my ring and started to weep. I just started wailing. I cried deep down to my core again. I felt it deep; my ribs ached. I couldn't contain myself. I felt like I had just lost everyone that was important to me at the same time. Like they had all been on the same plane that went down immediately after take off. I was a wreck.

I was not strong enough to face other people so I called off from work for the rest of the week. I called my boss and left a message on his voicemail. To my benefit, I was sounding like I truly was sick. All the crying had made my eyes appear to be swollen shut. My nose was so stuffy that I sounded extremely congested.

I was finally able to get out of the car and made it to the front door and into the living room. As soon as I opened the door and came inside, I saw Trenton's buffet that went to our new dining room furniture and I started crying again.

A deep breath, another emotional breakdown and fifteen minutes later, I made it upstairs to my bedroom. I threw myself on the bed with the little strength I had left. I didn't even attempt to change my clothes. I just pulled the blue comforter over my head. Minutes later when I could no longer breathe, I resurfaced. A took a few deep breaths to regain my normal breathing patterns as I pondered my life.

I took that time to look around the bedroom at Trenton's belongings, which had been recently moved into my townhouse. We didn't live together; but with the wedding in a few months he had begun to move his stuff. I kicked one of his suitcases. I stubbed my toe and winced in pain.

Even in trying to get back at him, I was still the one who got hurt. I thought of going all *Waiting to Exhale* on him and lighting it up. I decided against it though. I wasn't going to jail for anybody. So instead, I took that time to figure out what I was going to do next.

One thing was for sure; Trenton was the past. I realized that in situations like this, either you wanted the man and were willing to do what's necessary to fix it or you didn't and then you have to move on. I decided almost instantly that I did not want Trenton any longer. Any man who did not realize the contribution that I made to their life was not the one for me. With that said, I had to move on.

Yet, I was perplexed. Move on, what did that mean? How would I find my way?

I am the way, the truth and the life. Seek me. I heard a still, small voice speaking to my heart.

I don't know why suddenly it was so easy for me to make the declaration that it was over. Two and a half years ago, I couldn't bring myself to do it. I believe that God had made it easy for me.

There were certainly enough signs over the years that I should have left him behind, but I had been stuck on stupid.

I was confident that it was over. I had no desire to go back to Trenton. After all I had done for him; he had the nerve to cheat on me. That was the straw that broke the camel's back. We were finished.

Just then, my home phone rang. I rolled over in my bed to grab the phone.

"Hello."

"Hey girl, where you at?" It was Tracey, a friend from work. We had actually gone to college around the same time but never really knew each other but since working at the firm, we had gotten really cool. It was almost as if she always knew exactly when to call.

"Home, you do realize you called my house phone right?"

"Yeah, you're right. But you could have forwarded your phone to your cell phone. Don't act like that's not how you do." I could tell she was smiling.

"I guess but where would I be this late?"

"Duh, you do have a fiancé."

"Yeah, you're right."

"What's up, you sound all happy?"

"Nothing. I just got home from the mall. You know shopping is my life's joy."

"Girl, I don't know anyone else who spends as much time as you at the mall."

"What? It's always bargains. You know I don't pay full price for anything."

"I know. You are the queen of stretching a dollar. What did you get this time?"

"I spent $20 at Old Navy and I got about forty items. I even have something for you."

"Thanks."

"You wear a size eight, right?"

"You got it."

"What are you doing home tonight? I thought Wednesday was usually date night."

"Girl, you have a good memory. It is. But Trenton had a late meeting." I lied.

I wasn't quite ready to spill the beans.

"Oh, well good. Sometimes we need a little space." As she talked, my mind to wander to all the space I now had.

"Right, I do." I faked a yawn. "Well, I am tired. I'm going to get some sleep. We still on for lunch tomorrow?"

I knew that getting off the phone quickly would ensure that I did not write a check that my heart wasn't ready to cash. I was still so embarrassed, I mean it had only been a few hours since my life changed forever, again.

"You know it; I will call *La Tolteca* in the morning to make the reservation." Tracey loved her some Mexican. I loved it too; but it didn't love me.

"Okay, I'll talk to you tomorrow." With that, I hung up the phone.

I was so wrong; I knew good and well she wouldn't see me that next day. I just couldn't bring it up when I had finally gotten the tears to stop pouring from the windows of my soul. I would tell her soon.

As I drifted off to sleep that night, I couldn't help but wonder why this was happening to me.

I just kept asking myself out loud, "How did I get here?"

I couldn't help but pray to God that He would save me from the pain in my heart. But I knew that I had to go through this.

That which does not kill me will make me stronger, I told myself.

I knew that there was a reason why; my heart just didn't understand it yet. Everything that I had known for three years was gone. It had been here one minute and gone the next. I tried to settle my mind and get some rest as the next day was going to be tough enough.

As I tried to fall into a deep dream state, I started taking a hard look at my life. The images were so vivid and bright. Was there something that I could have done differently to prevent this from happening?

I took a hard, painful look at my past, which had led me to this moment. The past is hard to deal with but it is very necessary. My mind drifted back, way back to the beginning.

Chapter 4

For I know the plans I have for you, declares the Lord. Plans to prosper you and not harm you, plans to give you hope and a future.

Jeremiah 29:11

Born in the mid-seventies in the Riverside projects of Wilmington, Delaware, I was a product of two people caught up in the struggle. My mother, who had a 7th grade education and PHD from the streets, found a way to survive despite all that life threw her way. By the time she was 15, she had delivered her first-born child. Her parents threw her out of their home and prevented her from raising her first daughter. Drugs became her way to numb the pain; killing her softly and making her do anything to keep that high going.

My father was a militant cat who, although book smart, did not have the street smarts to prevent himself from getting caught in the crossfire of drugs. He could look the part as he accepted his college degree as one of the first African-American engineering graduates from the University of Delaware on the last day of May in the year I was born. But those who knew him, really knew him, knew of the demons living on the inside fighting their way to the surface.

My mom learned that she was pregnant with me when she was six months into her pregnancy. She went to her doctor's office complaining of daily heartburn and learned of my pending arrival. A month and a half later while having a bowel movement, I was almost born in the toilet.

I was given an uncommon name because my mom said when she looked at me she knew instantly that there was something different about me and she wanted me to live life realizing that I was unique.

She would often say, "There is nothing common about you."

Although I was her third child, she would tell you that there was nothing about her pregnancy with me that was like anything she had ever experienced with any of her other seven children. She never gained any weight; she didn't show, and when she gave birth, she had the belly of a woman three to four months pregnant.

She wasn't prepared for my entry into the world. But she knew when she held and nursed me that I was going to do big things. She knew that I would find a way to let the world know who I was.

On those rare occasions as a child when we would get a private moment, she would always say, "you are my dreamer. You're going to do something big."

I remember that as clear as a bright sunny day. One time in particular, I remember that we were walking to the corner store to get some penny candy. She was holding my hand and we were singing the name song.

I asked her, "Mommy, how did I get my name?"

I asked mostly because as a child, I was berated for my name. I definitely did not come to appreciate it until much later in life.

She answered, "I gave you a name like no one else because the Lord showed me that you would exist in this world like no one else. You won't understand this until later, but God has placed a special anointing on you. You will have an important job to do for God someday. Baby, always dream and never let anyone tell you that you can't."

"Mommy, what's anointing?"

"It's hard to explain but trust me, baby, it's a good thing."

At the age of six, I just smiled because she was definitely talking way over my head. Years later in Ms. Dixon's class in the sixth grade, I learned that my name means "a secret place where dreamers go to dream." And even then, I thought that was a cool meaning and not much else.

I think that was my proudest moment that day, walking with my mom to the corner store. I felt secure, I felt like I would always be safe. I don't know where my siblings were that day, but I remember clearly that it was Mommy and I having a special moment. That was one of our last.

Very soon thereafter, my life changed forever.

Chapter 5

You will be secure, because there is hope; you will look about you and take your rest in safety.

Job 11:18

During my eighth birthday party, the police raided my mother's home and confiscated her and enough drugs to start a local cartel. They chose my birthday slumber party. My parents had been divorced for a few years at that time and we lived with my mother.

I had been so exited to have my little friends over to celebrate my birthday and we were drawing our celebration to a close.

She had a boarder that was involved in drug trafficking and he was the reason for the raid. Police had been watching him and gotten a tip that he had a big shipment that had just come in. Mommy, although not responsible for the drugs in her home, got caught up because it was her home and they could not prove to whom the drugs belonged. And since she, too, was in the game, and under surveillance, they both got jail time.

I remember all of my little friends and I crying hysterically as the cops barged into and ransacked the house. We had just gotten finished eating our cereal when there was a loud boom at the front door and about ten men dressed in black holding guns barged in. We all screamed at the top of our lungs.

I remember going to live with my father very soon there after because my mom had to go away. She was incarcerated for, in my mind, my most important years. During those years, I needed a mother's influence. Although technically I had my stepmother, it wasn't the same because at that time my stepmother did not offer any positive influence in my life.

I was sixteen years old when my mother got out of jail. And when she got out, she left the state. So even then, there was no time to get to know her. She was like an aunt or uncle that we only saw during family reunions.

For a long time, I hated her for what she did to me. She wasn't there for me when I needed her most and I resented her for that. I actually thought that she went to jail to keep from taking care of us. I had heard of her struggles early on and how the struggle had her shackled. I am sure it had to be hard fighting for your right to a decent life with five kids at the age of 26.

I convinced myself that she had had enough and decided that if she went away, she would be relinquished of her motherly duties. As children, we have an immature way of rationalizing things. I told myself repeatedly year after year that she didn't want me. I gave myself headaches and serious bouts with nausea because I internalized her untimely departure from my life. When she left, my self-hatred intensified.

I must admit a part of me was grateful that my dad handled his responsibility and took custody of me. Otherwise, I could have become a ward of the state. It was not easy living with my father either but at least my brother, sister and I were together. My dad was not use to having three children around but he held his own. We had some good times before my dad married *her*. What I loved the most was that there was no more abuse. I felt secure. I felt like finally, I would be able to find out what my place in this cruel and unusual world would be. I was so wrong.

Once my dad took a new wife, the house where I lived became a battleground. There was always some form of contention; the dynamic of the house changed. All of a sudden there was constant competition for my father's affection and attention. With her around, it was always her versus us.

Who could get the love of my father?

Unfortunately, he didn't know how to share it evenly. He didn't know how to give it at all. He came from a family where the love was understood but not spoken. He expected his house to reflect the same, but it didn't.

My house was not a home; it was a combat zone. I had to fight for the right to exist positively in all the chaos that was my "family." In my opinion, we were five people in the same house with the same last name. We were angry; we were mad at each other all the time.

My stepmother separated us from our extended family because she was able to manipulate my father. I had nowhere to turn for solace. We only had one another and that was depressing. I hated the people I lived with, including myself. I was so angry. I was volatile. The pain and anguish that was my life had me shackled to an existence that I was anxiously waiting to break away from.

My dad traveled a lot for work and when he would leave, she would find reasons for us to get beatings and punished upon his return. My dad was a very hard man but my step-mom made him even worse, at least towards us. She had a way of pitting us against each other that made my dad grab his big leather belt and swing. The welts that bruised my skin also bruised my ego.

A new form of being abused found me; the physical pain caused emotional scarring that cut me deep. I had been cut so deep that it would take years to get out of that hell in my mind. The physical anguish of the beatings was bad. The mental torment that accompanied the lashings as well as the verbal insults from my stepmother harmed my spirit and wounded my pride. The tingling of my coarse skin was temporary but the thought of being inadequate and not equipped for my father's love lingered. The physical pain would eventually dissipate; but the emotional damage was hard to stomach.

Would I ever be enough? I often asked myself.

I started working as early as they would let you, back then it was at the age of thirteen and I began to handle my own personal affairs. I started buying the clothes I wanted and started saving to get a car when I turned sixteen.

I did whatever I could to get out of the house. I looked forward to the day I would ride off into the sunset in a car brought with my own hard-earned money. Nothing was handed to me. I busted my behind to get everything I had. It was all worth it. What I learned along the way has shaped my existence today.

My first job was at McDonald's. I worked there for four years. My dad & I opened a checking account at Wilmington Trust so that I could learn the importance of saving. He made me put half of each check in the bank. By the time I was 16 and ready to drive, I had over $5,000 in the account. Because I was a minor when the account was opened, my dad's name had to be listed on it. I never saw the monthly statements. One day, I did not have cheerleading practice and got home before my dad. I opened the first statement I had seen in over a year and found out that the balance was under $200. My dad had stolen my hard-earned money to get high. Even worse, when I confronted him, his response was that I owed him for all the years that he had taken care of me.

"Dad, I have a question for you."

"What's up, turkey?"

"I just got my bank statement and I don't understand it. The account says I only have $203 but I put over $400 in last month. Can you take me to the bank to resolve this?"

"No, that won't be necessary." He cleared his throat. "I took the money. I had a need and I took it."

"But it was my money dad. Why would you do that?" I mustered between my growing tears.

"You have been living here for years and that was your payment. Don't look at me like that."

If I had been allowed to hit my father I would have. I couldn't believe his lackadaisical attitude to spending my money. "What did you spend it on?"

"When you start paying the cost to be the boss, I will let you know."

But I knew. I wasn't stupid. I knew my dad got high. He would leave on Friday for work and we'd see him again on Monday after work.

What happened to taking care of me because he loved me? I wondered.

My psyche continued to try to find a place for me; a place where I would be safe without any type of abuse. I desperately wanted a place where love would abound.

When he stole my money without so much as an "I'm sorry," I moved Heaven and earth and really focused. I got straight A's and got over 1200 on my SAT so that I could get away.

I had to get away; there was no way I could continue to thrive in the hell in which I lived. You know how it is when you are around people who are stifling your growth? That is how I felt. My environment was a damnation to my soul.

As it turned out, away ended up being down the street at the University of Delaware because they offered me a full scholarship with a stipend and computer. All the other schools only wanted to pay a part of the tuition or room and board. But down on campus was far enough to make my escape.

I finished those four years only coming home once and as soon as I graduated, I had my first apartment lined up and the following year, I bought my first home. I was well on my way to getting onto something bigger and better, I just knew it. I was finally starting to pick up the decayed pieces of my broken life. But I still didn't love myself.

My father never told me that he loved me when I was growing up. I guess he assumed it was inferred because we had a roof over our head, food on the table and clothes on our backs. I was over 25 years old by the time that he ever actually said those three words. Hearing those words could have changed my whole life. I would have felt the worth that could have reshaped my self-esteem and led me to a place of confidence without the entire struggle I had to endure to get there years later and on my own. Additionally, there would not have been a need for me to go out and find love in all the wrong places.

As a young girl, having a father who shows you the way that you deserve to be treated is paramount. All subsequent male-female relationships are shaped by that first and very important relationship and I never had that with my dad. No one ever showed me my value. Love and belief were never poured into me so that I would never settle for anything less than what I deserved. So in turn, I thought I deserved nothing special, just the ordinary, run of the mill things in life. And that is what I got. Remember, life and death lies in the power of the tongue. My tongue spoke death because I didn't know any better.

My family truly shaped my existence. I am who I am because I come from where I come from. I learned to hustle and survive with strength because of my parents. I developed my addictions and idiosyncrasies from them. I learned conviction and struggle from watching them. I learned right from wrong with them as my example. I believe that my need to survive and go over, under and around the obstacles in my life comes from my mother.

My thirst for knowledge and perfectionist attitude comes from my father. I, too, never let the world into my microcosm because I learned how to be fully functional like my father. I was a chameleon. I changed my colors to suit the crowd and no one was the wiser that I was just pretending to be what they saw when they looked at me.

I was my mother's third child and my father's second. I have one whole brother and one whole sister. On my mom's side, I also have one half-sister and one half-brother. My mother also had a set of twins that no one, including her, ever talks about. My dad also has a son from his second marriage.

Growing up, I did not have a close or strong relationship with any of my siblings. I was left alone a lot because I was different and often accused of thinking I was better than them. I was told that I was a "white girl," trying to act like I was better. I didn't feel like I was better but I must admit, I wanted more than what we had.

Fake it until you make it, I always told myself. I had a dream deferred and it was bound to explode.

I didn't want to be a drug addict or have a bunch of babies by different men. That was all you saw in my community. I had so many cousins and friends who had three or more children and three and more baby's daddies by the time they were sixteen or seventeen years old.

I didn't smoke or drink; I wanted nothing to do with anything that resembled substance abuse. I wanted more. I knew that more existed. It had to get better. I was committed to getting away from the struggle.

I remember my dad instilling in me through fear and watching him and others in and around my family, that education was my key out of this environment. I made it my business to excel in school. I had a thirst for knowledge because it was my insurance policy out of the fiery furnace that was my life.

I was always trying to find a way to escape and lose myself in someone else's existence. I would write short stories where I was amongst people who loved and cared about me. I always sought relationships with people who had amazing families.

I avoided as many holiday meals as possible with my family. I made it my business to stay away from that capricious environment as much as I could.

I was always dreaming and exploring my creative side. I always wanted to write and enjoyed English class the most throughout school. There was something about the possibility of language that made me come alive. I knew that in my mind, I could create a place where love truly would conquer all. My journals became my way out of the hell in which I lived.

The best part about my journal was that I never had to move from the battleground to experience solace.

I was left alone a lot, which made me independent minded. No one ever checked to see if I need anything so I learned early that "if it was to be, it was up to me." That mantra later turned into a disastrous self-centered perception that kept everyone who wanted to get to know me at bay because they thought I was not approachable. I had a wall like that of Jericho around my life. I had determined that when I let others in, they hurt me so unless I could find an inherent need for you in my life, I did not let you get close enough to attach shackles to my mind, body or spirit. There is however, an exception to every rule and mine was men.

Chapter 6

You only have I chosen of all the families of the earth; therefore I will punish you for all your sins.

Amos 3:2

As I turned over, I remembered another key to unlocking my past.

It was very dark in the room; I could barely see the shape that was progressively coming toward me. I could hear his voice. It was raspy. It sounded like he was speaking from behind a cloth; it was garbled and broken. He stumbled and stammered over his words frequently. I am not sure if it was fear or a speech impediment. But he kept repeating the commands over and over.

"Get down on your knees."

"Move faster."

There was soft music playing. The music was almost hypnotizing. It calmed me down. He gave me something to drink. It tasted and smelled funny but it made me tingle and giggle.

His hands were cold and his breath was thick. His hair always smelled funny, like Sulfur 8 hair grease. He always had candles burning and they scared me. The thought of him touching me with those cold hands made me shudder. I cringed at the memory. It made me want to vomit.

I remembered asking him to stop. I remembered saying no. He kept going and he took what he came for.

I was sexually abused as a child. I have been healed of the emotional, physical and psychological scars (thanks to God); therefore, I see no need to share the identity of this man. I was seven years old when it started; it went on for at least a year.

He was always telling me how much he loved me, and if I loved him it would be our little secret, something special to be shared just between us. I trusted this man. He was always fun and when he came to visit, he always had presents or cash for candy from the penny store. I didn't suspect a thing when he wanted to take me to the park in his car one day when he saw me walking home from the store.

He made me believe that all little girls did this with their "uncles." He told me that I was not going to get birthday or Christmas presents if we didn't have our special time. He told me that he loved me and that I was the most important little girl in his life. He told me that he would do anything for me. I was his special girl. I was the apple of his eye.

He threatened me and told me that if I ever told anyone, I would get hurt and he didn't want to hurt me. But he would if I told the secret.

Our little secret, I shivered at the thought.

I recollect, even at that age, feeling that it was wrong for me to be engaged in these activities but he led me to believe that it was okay to do what we did. I felt worthless, dirty and ashamed whenever I was alone with him.

How could it be okay if it felt so wrong?

I recall shivering with the pain, angst, anxiety and fear that if I said something he *really* would kill me.

I asked myself why I had been the chosen one. To this day, I don't understand what a man would want with a girl.

But the gifts kept coming and as a little girl, they pacified me enough to keep our little secret. I cried myself to sleep as I struggled to erase the vivid memories of his face and hands coming toward me.

He always told me I was beautiful and special. He said that only special girls got to spend special time with him and that I should be proud that he thought I was special.

I tried to cut my face so that I wouldn't be beautiful anymore. I got a beating by my mom for trying to hurt myself.

"Why did you do this?" She screamed at me.

"It was an accident Mommy. I didn't mean it." I wouldn't dare tell her for fear that he would find out and hurt me.

But I did mean it. I didn't want to be beautiful. In my mind, beauty was dirty and embarrassing. I wanted to make my face ugly. If being considered beautiful was grounds to be touched in places and coerced into dirty acts, I did not want it.

I don't know if she would have believed me anyway. There were times when she put men before us. After all, he was *her* friend.

Similarly, I remember both an older male and female cousin molesting me. They, too, told me that I was special.

For years, I hated when people called me special, it always sent me back to that dark place. I would instantly change my demeanor when a teacher told me that I was special. I never wanted to be special if special meant that I would be subjected to an inclusion into a sin beyond my understanding. I had been robbed. They stole my opportunity to look at life through a little girl's eyes.

My father was not there to protect me and secure my innocence. For years, I hated my father because as a little girl, I was plagued with insecurities about why I was chosen for these horrible acts. I abhorred my parents and believed that they didn't love me enough to protect me and prevent my innocence from being stolen. I never told anyone but somehow I thought that they should know that something was going on with their little girl. Because they never figured it out, I blamed them for not loving me enough. If they loved me more, they would have been able to sense that something was not right and seek to find out what it was so that their little girl would feel protected and secure.

Naturally, because my innocence was clouded by his perversion, I thought that love and physical intimacy was the same thing. I thought the only way you could show a man that you loved him was to be physically intimate with him. Therefore, I became promiscuous at an early age.

I did consent to knowing the pleasures of a man for the first time at thirteen years old because some little boy across the park told me he loved me. I believed him and because I associated love with physical intimacy, I gladly gave him a cookie from my cookie jar. Honestly, and I am not proud of it, but I gave out my fair share of cookies.

I used my cookies as a means to be wanted, loved and appreciated. I got my "high" from getting physical and I imagined it to be much like that of a crack addict. I was after all my parents' daughter. That next "hit" would be the one to take me to the next level. My next level was love and acceptance. I wanted terribly to finally belong somewhere.

I longed for a place where my mother didn't abandon me. I was hoping for a place where the people I trusted didn't steal my innocence. I would have given anything for a place where my father didn't entrust me to a woman who often wished I wasn't there. More than ever, I longed for a place where family members didn't touch me inappropriately. A place where I would know true love, a love that takes away all pain, was a longstanding prayer on my list. I was desperate for a love that didn't hurt. I yearned to know a love that was complete with acceptance and power. What I got instead was self-hate, disgust, and personal contempt.

For years, I sought solace in the comforts of a man. As I looked back over my life, I learned that love's existence had nothing to do with those comforts; the love I desired lived some place deeper. I never realized that it was wrong. I thought it was okay because I had been made into a "woman" at a tender age when that first man had his way with me. In order to keep myself from going crazy, I changed the meaning of it and did my best to take the horrible thoughts, memories and emotions away. I attempted to use physical intimacy as a way to gain control and find the love that had always been missing in my life.

The bottom line: I didn't know my worth. Not knowing my worth put me in a position where I was willing to compromise. I lost myself in hopes that my worth was in the palm of a man's hand. That feeling immobilized and prevented me from knowing who I was and realizing all that I could become. I got so caught up; so addicted to finding my worth that I was willing to make casual covenants in order to find it. I dealt with fear, shame and guilt simultaneously hoping that the next man would be the man to truly make me feel like my life had value. I was desperately seeking someone to tell me that I was incredible, to tell me that I was amazing.

As it turned out, I was disappointed when I realized that all he wanted was a cookie from my cookie jar. And what's worse, I usually gave him one.

I had convinced myself that Trenton was that man. I kept telling myself that Trenton was the one to finally break the cycle and love me the way a man should love a woman. I promised myself that one day when he got himself together and realized that I was a great person not his doormat, he would love me and love me right. And that day would finally make right all the wrongs I had endured along the way.

But I had been wrong. Trenton was now the past; there was a new day dawning and the best was yet to come.

Chapter 7

As for me, I watch in hope for the Lord. I wait for God my Savior; my God will hear me.

Micah 7:7

When the sun opened my eyes Thursday morning prematurely, I immediately looked down at the engagement ring that was still on my slender and delicate finger. Then I shook my head. I just couldn't believe that this had happened. How did I, this loyal puppy, get hoodwinked into believing that this time would be different? I was exactly the same; the issues of my past were plaguing me yet I was naive enough to believe that the results would change. That, I later learned, is the definition of insanity.

I felt like I was in a hot, sticky, syrupy and stifling haze. It was so thick that I couldn't breathe through my nose. I felt as if my eyes had been swollen shut, and it hurt to move my lips just to moisten my mouth. I shifted my weight trying to get comfortable. I had a long night of tossing and turning before I found enough peace to sleep and when I finally settled in, the sun woke me.

I looked down at my engagement ring again and sighed.

Was this worth all the trouble? I thought.

"No, hell no." I said out loud. It wasn't worth all of this. How had I missed the key signs that this would happen?

Looking at it disgusted me. I twisted the ten carat yellow gold band with a half-carat marquise cut center diamond from my finger and hurled it across the room; it landed on my maple wood colored dresser after bouncing off the matching mirror.

Habitually, I grabbed my cell phone off the nightstand and turned it on. I had fifteen new messages. I didn't need to take the time to check them; they were from Trenton. I turned my cell phone right back off.

Not today, I thought to myself and turned back over. "It is over." I said confidently.

I let out a deep breath and I shook my head. I remembered back to when I first met Trenton.

I was working in the customer service department when he and a group of management trainees walked in looking for a place to sit to get some work done. Since I was working in a specialty unit, we had lots of extra seats. He kept coming over to me with questions. Mind you, these were questions that he, a management trainee, should have known the answers to. I just ignored his obvious flirting because I wasn't feeling him. Day after day, he asked questions. I could tell he liked me. He wasn't my type. First of all, he was just about my height and my ideal guy was at least six foot two. He was also corny and tried too hard. In my opinion, a man who tried that hard had something to hide.

Why hadn't I listened to my own inner rationale? The first instinct is always the correct one, I thought as I reflected.

But all of a sudden he was everywhere. If I went to a networking event after work, I ran into Trenton. At the Young Professionals Urban League meetings, you guessed it, I saw Trenton. I even saw him at the gym once. I mean, between work and all of my extra activities, he was everywhere. He was like a credit card; it was almost as if I didn't leave home without him.

I remember the first time we had a conversation unrelated to work, I thought he seemed like a nice enough guy. He kind of followed me around from picture to picture at an African American Art exhibit at the DCCA trying to find a reason to get my opinion on each piece. That was kind of cute at first, but even that got old.

He's too short for me, I kept telling myself. I never wanted to look at my man eye to eye; I always had a vision of looking up to the man in my life. I think that was largely due to the fact that my dad was about six foot three and not to mention all the "tall, dark and handsome" clichés in the world. Trenton was dark, very dark and he did have a bright white smile. Handsome, I think he started to grow on me. After months of running into him, I figured we could be friends.

Then that February, I ran into him again in Kmart and suddenly, he looked different. He had shaved his head bald and it did wonders for him. I think it even made him look taller. He had obviously gotten someone to help him change his image because he didn't look drab anymore. All of a sudden, he looked real good. And he asked me out. And I said yes. What the heck…what did I have to lose? I had definitely watched *Love Jones* on enough Friday nights to let him take me to dinner.

As I thought back to where we started, I recalled that in the beginning, he was amazing. He was just what the doctor ordered. He was considerate, attentive, kind, honest, loving and respectful. Isn't that the way it always is when a relationship starts? Not to mention that he had what I desperately craved, a great family.

My thoughts were interrupted; the phone rang. I knew it was Tracey; it was 9 am.

"Why did your secretary just tell me that you weren't in today?"

"Because I am not, I decided to take the day off. I was going to call you in a little while."

"Well, why aren't you here? You know I like to get my morning pancakes with you!"

I had to laugh, that was Tracey. She could always draw a smile.

"I just couldn't face people today. Last night was too much." I let my secret slip out. I couldn't hold water. I really wasn't ready to have this conversation yet, but ready or not…

"Didn't we talk last night? You sounded okay when we talked. Did something happen after that? You know you can talk to me. I am here for you no matter what."

With those words, I lost it. I did really feel like I could talk to her. She was one of those friends that never stood in judgment of me. I sighed as tears flooded and stung my eyes, my voice got a bit higher and I told her. I told her the abridged version of what had happened in about thirty seconds.

"Trenton confessed that he got some old lady pregnant and the wedding is off!"

"Did you say old lady? Shut your mouth. What? Wait, What? Trenton. I didn't think he had it in him. That's just nasty!"

What she said made me laugh. I chuckled.

"Girl, you're so crazy."

That was Tracey. There was always a reason to laugh when you were in her presence. That was truly one of the things I loved about her personality.

"Well, you're able to laugh, that's a good sign. Seriously, how are you feeling?" She asked with clear concern in her voice. I could tell she wasn't sure exactly what to say. I guess I couldn't blame her; what would I have said to a friend if the shoe was on the other foot?

"Well, I am making it. Highs and lows come and go. But the bottom line is that it is over. Right now, I am just trying to sort through his stuff and get all memories of him out of my house."

"Is that a good idea to do right now?"

I could hear her concern.

"Girl, it's got to go. If I keep looking at it, it will drive me insane. If it stays, I'll be recreating *Waiting to Exhale* up in here. I've been playing the CD on repeat since last night."

And it hurts like hell, I said inwardly as the song poured from my speakers.

"Well, don't do that. Okay, what can I do? When did this happen? Do you want to meet for lunch?"

"No, girl thanks, I can't go anywhere today. I look tore up from the floor up. I have so much to sort through. But you can pray for me, girl. Pray my strength."

"Oh, you know I will do that. Also, what are you doing on Sunday?"

"I don't have any plans, why? What's up?"

"Well, why don't you come to church with me? I know you are not going back to Trenton's church."

"I know that's right." I thought for a second and then I answered, "Okay, I will."

Tracey had invited me to her church several times before but I had always made one excuse after another. I knew that she went to a church where the Holy Spirit ran high and I didn't know if I was ready for that kind of experience with the Lord.

But I definitely wasn't going back to Trenton's church and I also no longer felt comfortable going to the church I belonged to prior to joining Trenton's church, so I agreed to visit her church. I was actually excited for a different experience and perhaps a true encounter with God.

And if God was going to get me through this, I had to start by going to where He was and He was definitely at a spirit-filled church.

"Yeah, I'll go to your church. I need directions though," I repeated, as I felt better and better about committing to attend service with her, finally.

"Oh, it's easy. I'll call you Saturday and give them to you. Better yet, let's have breakfast and I'll print them out for you. Just know now that we start at 10:29."

"10:29?" I asked. I knew there had to be a story to match that statement.

"Yeah, my Pastor is all about timeliness. If you want to be there when it all begins, you better be early because the Holy Ghost party gets started at 10:30 on the dot." She chuckled, but I knew she was dead serious.

"Deal, now let me get back to my workload. See you on Saturday," I rushed off the phone. If I stayed on, I would want to talk and rehash it over and over. That would not do anyone any good.

Trust me. I will do exceedingly; abundantly above all you could ever ask of or think. I heard a whisper cross my shoulders. It gave me chills. I shook it off and finished my conversation with Tracey.

She said, "Okay, but if you need me before then, call me. I'm never too busy to lend an ear."

Chapter 8

Come to me, all you who are weary and burdened, and I will give you rest. Take my yoke upon you and learn from me, for I am gentle and humble in heart and you will find rest for your souls. For my yoke is easy and my burden is light.

Matthew 11:28-30

I spent the rest of the week in and out of consciousness. I had so much to do. I had to make a doctor's appointment to get tested for all the sexually transmitted diseases and of course HIV. I did not trust that Trenton and Constance were clean. I didn't know where she had been.

And maybe Trenton had even dipped with others. There was no way for me to know for sure so I had to get myself checked out. I was concerned because there were those few times when I gave in to his incessant begging giving him five minutes to do his thing and even with using condoms you can't be too sure. I couldn't take any chances; my life was just beginning and I didn't want it halted because of someone else's indiscretions, when I had been so careful during my own. I couldn't believe that I was in this place; I know I keep saying that but it is the truth. I couldn't get my arms around the facts of the matter.

My mind was racing; there was so much to do. I had to cancel reservations and arrangements that were being made for the wedding. I was supposed to meet the florist the day after his confession.

I needed to get the items that I had purchased together and get them ready to go back to the stores. I was returning everything that I could. I wanted as much of my money back as possible. I needed to call the girls in the wedding, all 10 of them, to let them know the wedding was off. I really wasn't ready to face the music.

But if I was going to face it, I was going to look my best. When my funk was over, I was getting a hair cut, and I was going to use my wedding funds to buy me my dream car. I was going to get a new attitude and while I was healing, I was at least going to be the best looking jacked up girl in Delaware.

I felt sick to my stomach at the thought that I had even arrived at this destination. I had staked so much on Trenton. I had put him on a pedestal and made him my "savior" and that was the worse thing that I could've done as I now realized it.

I started thinking back to a time when life was good and Trenton and I were together and happy.

Yeah, the early days of our relationship were off the chart. Trenton invited me home to meet his parents after we'd been dating for two weeks. I was so nervous. I hadn't met too many families in my past relationships. I was nervous for no reason; his mom loved me. We had so much in common. And he had sisters, which I thought would be even more nerve wrecking. Surprisingly, we hit it off famously.

I loved his family instantly. They were warm, friendly and loving. They were good people. They were so accepting and they focused on making me a part of the family, right away. Coming from my background, I was so comfortable. I exchanged numbers with his two sisters and we became fast friends. We started to go visit his family every other weekend.

They were in Northern Pennsylvania, about an hour and a half away. We would tear the highway up and get there sometimes in about an hour and ten minutes, especially when I was driving.

One of the things I loved about Trenton was his family and how close they were. He knew exactly how to make me feel at ease. I felt completely comfortable with them and that made a huge difference and removed a lot of pressure. From time to time, I still miss the Petersons.

We started to spend every waking moment together. We had plenty of those nights on the phone for so many hours that eventually we were listening to each other breathe and it was okay. Neither of us wanted to hang up. It was that sweet puppy love that made everything all right with the world. We were together in everyway that we could be, every moment that we could be. On the phone, in person, instant messaging on AOL or MSN, if we could be in contact, we were.

The flowers kept coming; the sweet nothings kept my ears tickled and my heart light. I was happy. For the first time in a long time, I was truly happy. I was in love. My cup was full. And it was all because of him. I must admit, I did love me some Trenton. Trenton in the morning, Trenton in the noonday and Trenton in the evening. It may have taken me a while to warm up to him but once I did, I was cooking with gas.

I had my best Valentine's Day ever that year. We met just in the knick of time. He took me to dinner at the Hotel DuPont in Wilmington. It was beautiful. It was a very expensive hotel and restaurant. The DuPont's were one of the oldest and richest families in the state of Delaware and it was a big deal to dine at any of their properties. Their family went as far back as Thomas Jefferson. He and Pierre DuPont conducted a lot of business together. The lobbies and restaurants were so picturesque. The old-world tapestries and rich, vibrant colors demonstrated the amount of money that the DuPont family had.

The restaurant where we dined that night had hues of deep gold, burgundy and hunter green. It was so beautiful.

To seal the night in love and luxury, Trenton bought me two-dozen red, white and yellow roses.

As he presented them, he said, “The yellow roses are for our friendship, which I pray will continue to grow. The white roses are for the purity of what we are building and the red roses are for the passion that is already growing inside of me.”

I could have melted into a puddle right there. That was the most beautiful thing anyone had ever said to me. I didn’t get out much but I was so happy. I hugged him as my eyes swelled with big fat tears.

“That was so beautiful. Thank you so much for an amazing Valentine’s Day.”

It had just begun and I already knew that it would be the best one I had ever had. It was. To this day, I have not had a Valentine’s Day that could come close to the first one we shared.

We enjoyed a superb dinner and then we went back to my house. It was that night that we first sealed our bond with the purest, unyielding encounter of bodies intertwined. It was very special. He made me feel so warm and loved. It was the first time that I had felt that the person that I was with was more concerned about me than his own needs.

The next morning, we woke to my alarm, which was set to the radio and Tyrese’s song *Sweet Lady* was playing. He turned towards me and asked me to be his Sweet Lady. I said yes immediately. We became a couple and that became our song. Up until a few years ago, hearing that song sent a shrill twinge down my back.

He looked at me and breathed me in with his seductive bedroom eyes and asked, "Can I see how you taste first thing in the morning?"

I didn't even hesitate to lean into him and seal our new relationship.

Things were progressing well. We never argued or disagreed about anything. We were in the honeymoon phase of our relationship. For the first time, I felt that I had met a man that was on my level and that we could grow together. Trenton was exactly nine months older than me. He use to always say that I was born for him. There was a time when I truly believed that.

We were together about six months, when Trenton decided that he was quitting his job at the firm to start his own business. I must admit; I was not pleased. I was nervous as I thought of him striking out on his own without a sound business concept.

One thing I always remembered was when my dad said, "You don't quit one hustle until the next one is up and running."

I had read the business plan. It was not a good one. But what does a good woman do? She supports her man. So I re-read the plan and offered suggestions to make it more viable. I challenged him to make key changes that would secure the future of his consulting firm. He took each suggestion but never said thank you. I helped him build his website. I proofread the copy before he published it. I was his wordsmith. I gave him just the right words.

I believed in him and no matter what, that was enough for me.

With my help, his business plan got noticed and he was able to secure his first contracts. I was his marketing coordinator. I never got a thank you. I couldn't even get business cards.

I was so nervous about him not having job security. One of the things I liked about him when we met was that he had a future in business. He didn't have the sharpest mind but he learned quickly. He took criticism well and made changes to better himself. I could always respect that. I felt like he missed the writing on the walls telling him that his company would not last and in two years he would be back in the job market. Only this time, he would be screwed because he walked away from a company that was going to pay him to grow into a sound businessman. He had business partners, but neither of them was making the commitment he was and quitting their jobs. But Trenton had an ego problem. No one could suggest that he do something other than what he decided. It was no use. He thought he had all the answers.

The early stages of getting his company ready for "show time" put a huge strain on us. We began to fight over the stupidest things but none of the subject matter had anything to do with us. It became all about his business. I was the supportive girlfriend. I worked my day job, came home and did what he needed me to do to help. I did it even though I knew it was a bad idea. Like I said before, I stood by my man.

I know that my need to get acceptance by helping others stemmed from the fact that I wasn't told that I was loved as a child. Feeling betrayed at every turn, the pangs of loneliness taunted me so I would do anything to prevent that from happening. Because my father never showed emotion or told me that I was great, a feeling of insecurity was created within me.

As a result, I sought approval from everyone that gave me the slightest thought. I never wanted to be alone. I would do anything to prevent that. I would shake in fear like an epileptic at the thought of, at the end of the day, being alone. I can tell you honestly that this fear had trapped me and kept me bound to situations that I knew were not good for me. And with Trenton, there were so many signs that I should get out and run as fast as I could.

At this stage of the relationship I was already in love with Trenton so if he was going to quit his job and do his own thing, I was going to be right there with him, because that's how I do. In my mind, you go big or you stay home. I always went big. I fell big too.

I fell in love with him so fast and I fell hard. He *was* good to me. I got flowers weekly, lots of phone calls throughout the day and plenty of attention. He knew exactly what I needed to keep me just happy enough. That is such a powerful word.

I often asked myself "When do you endure enough to stir enough courage to walk away from a relationship that is only maintaining and not growing?"

Through this incident, I have learned that no one should settle for a situation that is just enough. I have learned that life is too short to settle. I knew early on in our relationship that I was settling for Trenton but I didn't believe that I had the strength needed to walk away. Past the flowers and the attention, his flaws were evident and they were significant enough to tell me he was not the one. But, I wanted the fairytale more than life itself. I wanted to get married and have children just so that I could prove that I could be part of a real family. I wanted this so bad that I was willing to be inconvenienced enough to get it. And since Trenton was already there...I could just change him...You know how we do, thinking we can change the man into who we want.

Chapter 9

Now we see but a poor reflection as in a mirror; then we shall see face to face. Now I know in part; then I shall know fully, even as I am fully known.

1 Corinthians 13:12

I can't lie. I did believe that I loved Trenton, especially in those early days. He was a good man. Just like they say, love is blind and it makes us do stupid things. Here's what love made me do.

My good friend had just had a baby and she was so in love and I looked at them, and I wanted what they had. She was such an amazing person that she deserved the love that she had. But I wanted it too. I admit I was envious. I felt like she had truly encapsulated what I wanted all of my life and it lied in her child. Because she and her man had created a new life based on their love it seemed as if they had gotten even closer. They got married just after the baby was born.

So brilliant me, after realizing that I had already missed two days worth of birth control pills, I decided not to "catch" up but instead, I stopped taking my pills in the middle of the pack. I wasn't sure if I could even get pregnant because I had been on the pill for so long. But one thing was for certain; I was willing to go against everything I believed in for "love" to find out. That is how powerful my need to be loved was. Scary, isn't it?

My belief about children was simple, just the way God intended it. To me, children were a blessing that was a part of the marriage union. I had watched enough single mothers who had babies and struggled without the father as a part of their children's lives to know that it wasn't for me. It was partly because I had always wanted to be a strong, solid family, that which I had been denied. Not that marriage was a surety, but it did invoke an amount of security and stability in the life of the child. And marriage, when entered into with God's blessing and intentions, would be blessed to weather the storms of life. And that was what I had dreamed of for so long. Granted, things happen but I didn't want to be a statistic and an unwed mother chasing a man down for child support.

I just wanted something different for myself. But again, Trenton made me carelessly abandon my morals. *What love makes us do?*

I had no idea if my scattered thought would even work; but it did. I got pregnant that September, after we had been together for seven months. I was ecstatic. I had done it; I had gotten pregnant.

I willingly abandoned everything I believed in at the thought of having Trenton's child. I was so in love and the thought that we were having a baby had me on cloud nine. I could hardly wait to tell Trenton.

The thought of having his baby had me so excited I felt on top of the world. We were creating someone together and that was magical; it was the kind of magic I dreamed and read about in those romance novels or saw in those old movies on TV. It was the kind of magic that I wanted in my life because my life was so full of anything but magic. From the moment I could remember doom surrounded me.

My life had always been so dark and finally there was light. Trenton was my light. With him I felt like I could do anything, we could do anything together. It was so great the way our love turned into the baby that was growing inside of me.

I put my hands on my belly and felt our love. I got caught up at the thought that we were going to be parents. I couldn't wait to see his face when he felt the love growing inside of me.

I had put all my stock into the idea that having a baby would cure the problems in our relationship. I was foolish enough to think that a baby would be like a magic wand, which would cure the problems in me. I had been so stupid; I was no better than those girls I use to berate for trying to trap a man. Here I was trying to do the same exact thing. Love dust clouded my vision and because I couldn't see clearly, I made a life-changing mistake.

I had planned out how I would let him know. I called him from work that day after I left the lab getting my confirmation blood test. The store bought test was correct; I was pregnant.

"Hey baby. You got any plans tonight?"

"Nope, why? What's up?"

"I just want to make my man dinner, that's all." I was smiling through the phone. I just knew he could hear the sun shining.

"Okay, you know I am always down for your cooking. What time should I get there?"

"Seven sharp."

"Okay, babe. I'll see you then. Do you need me to bring anything? I can pick up dessert if you like. At least let me grab a bottle of wine."

"No, thanks. I'll have everything we need," I gushed emphatically. I couldn't wait to see him. I was so excited. I just knew our night was going to be perfect.

I left work a little early so that I could run to the grocery store and beat the traffic from Wilmington to Bear. Once I got down to my area, I ran into the supermarket to gather up all I needed for Trenton's favorite meal. I was making T-bone steak, baked sweet potato and steamed broccoli with apple cobbler for dessert. I gathered up all the items I needed. I decided that I would toss a salad and get some French bread. Dinner was going to be perfect. I loved to cook; and when I cooked, Trenton was in Heaven.

I returned to the front of the store and started to scout out a checkout line. I got into a line with only two people ahead of me. I was psyched; I was making good time. I looked down at my cart to make sure that I wasn't missing anything. I went over the list in my head. Then I realized that I almost forgot to get the French vanilla ice cream. I ran back to the frozen food section from my place in the line. The lady behind me was not pleased when I asked her to excuse me. I think I heard her mumble something smart under her breath as I hurried past her, with a smile on my face. I didn't care; I wasn't even phased.

Nothing was going to wreck my flow that night. Nothing could deflate my balloon. Back to the line with the ice cream in hand, I started to load my groceries onto the conveyor belt. I paid for my goods and rushed back to my car. I put everything in the back seat because my trunk was a mess. I slid into the driver's seat; turned on the CD player and my girls Zhane instantly filled the car. I sang along, of course. "Sending my love to you, sealing it with a kiss…" I was just bopping along and before I knew it, I was in my driveway. Singing to Trenton as I drove made the ride go faster than normal.

I gathered up all the bags and headed towards the front door. I didn't have my keys ready so when I got there, I had to put the bags on the step. A quick search revealed that I didn't have my keys. I went back to the car where I could see my house key dangling.

I thought to myself, *if my head wasn't attached.*

I chuckled, grabbed my keys from the ignition; yes, the car was still running! I ran back to the door, opened it, grabbed up the bags and headed inside. I was still smiling as I plopped everything onto the kitchen table. I ran back to shut the door and then I grabbed an apron, washed my hands and got to work. It didn't take me long to get everything started before I ran upstairs to take a quick shower.

In the shower, I rubbed my stomach; then hugged my stomach to say "hi" to the life growing inside me. I smiled and quickly freshened up. I hummed and danced while I was in the shower and then jumped out and quickly toweled off. Once dry, I selected the perfect little black dress, chose my undergarments carefully then made myself cute. I put on a little bit of lip-gloss to make my lips look sexy and curled my hair the way Trenton loved it. I couldn't wait to see him.

I ran back down to the kitchen to check on everything, which was cooking up nicely. I went over to the stereo system and selected his favorite jazz CD, a Grover Washington Jr. compilation and set it up so that at the right moment, I could hit "play" on the remote. I was setting the mood and I just knew that once he arrived, he would be ready to go.

I set the table nicely. I put the fresh Gerber daisies and calla lilies I purchased at the store in my nicest vase in the center of the kitchen table. I got my *Ralph Lauren* placemats that matched the wedge wood blue walls in the kitchen perfectly. I got my finest plates and silverware out of the hutch in the basement and set out the champagne flutes. I grabbed the sparkling cider and allowed it to chill in the refrigerator until the perfect moment. Everything looked as peaceful as a summer day at sunset when I was all finished setting up.

I turned at the sound of Trenton's key opening the front door. He was prompt. I smiled like a kid in a penny candy store with two dollars, as he crossed the threshold.

"Baby!" I said as I ran into his arms. He was smiling just as hard as I.

"Hey sweetie, how are you? How was your day?" His smile intensified as he drew close to me.

"It was great! How was yours?"

"It was tough; my workload is getting harder to manage. But I am better now." He walked into the kitchen. "Wow, what is all this?" He turned to face me with a smile so big it looked as if he had one thousand teeth.

I smiled. "It's for us. I just wanted to do something special for you. Today, I felt your love so strongly. I got you a present." I reached in to give him another hug. I breathed him in. He spelled like *Cool Water*.

"Baby, you didn't have to get me anything. You are my present." He deepened our embrace.

"I know I didn't have to, but I wanted to. Open it." I handled him the small, neatly gift-wrapped box.

He removed the baby blue wrapping paper and revealed a small brown box. He looked up at me.

I smiled and winked at him. "Open it," I prodded. I couldn't wait for him to reveal the sterling silver rattle I had purchased that day from *Things Remembered.* Engraved on the rattle were the words "for our baby." It was the perfect gift. I could hardly contain myself; I had been waiting for this moment my whole life.

He looked down at the box, then back up at me and smiled. "This really isn't necessary. You are too much. I love you." With that, he reached over and kissed me gently on the cheek, then on the lips.

His lips were soft and warm, inviting me closer.

"Open it, I can't wait. If you don't do it, I will open it myself." I was growing so impatient; the suspense was killing me. I was living for his reaction.

"Okay, you know I like to get you fired up." He smiled gently and reached in to tickle me. I must admit; I loved his beautiful white smile. I successfully dodged his tickle attempt.

Then he lifted the lid off the box and peered inside. The smile on his face went limp.

"Do you like it?"

"I don't get it. What does this mean?"

I cut my espresso brown eyes at him. "Well, you know how I have been really tired and sleeping every moment that I can? I went to the doctor today and he confirmed what I was thinking. My breasts have been swollen and everyday at noon they hurt for about thirty minutes." I checked his face. It was lifeless.

Out with it, I told myself.

Suddenly I was nervous because he face was absent of emotion. "We are going to have a baby." I said, very excitedly. I felt like I was telling him that I had the winning ticket to the 65 million dollar *Powerball* lottery game.

Trenton said nothing. Instead, he picked up his car keys and walked towards the front door. "I'll be back. I need to think. Don't wait up." With that, he was gone.

I stood there for a few minutes stunned and unable to move. I woke up about five minutes later and looked at the door. He was gone. I felt the air slowly seeping out of my balloon. He needed to think?

What was there for him to think about?

Wow. I was flabbergasted; how could he be so selfish right now? I wanted to give him something to think about. I wanted to give him a piece of my mind.

I had cooked his favorite meal, prepared to rejoice over the blessing that we were being granted and he needed to think. I was going to bring his first-born child into this world and he needed to think. What kind of response was that? How could he think about himself right now? How could he walk out on me at a moment like this? Yes, I realize that our relationship was new and not void of issues, but we were having a baby. We'd been successful in creating a person that would represent a part of each of us.

He claimed to love me but love is not selfish. I was thoroughly confused. My head started to spin. I shook it off. I decided that since there was nothing I could do about the fact that he was gone, off to think, I would focus my efforts elsewhere. I shook my head a second time and went into the kitchen and put the food into the oven on warm. I probably should have just put everything in the trash. I no longer had an appetite.

As I opened the oven door, the heat enveloped my body and I caught a chill. I shivered before I erupted into tears. All of a sudden, the emotion overwhelmed me. The tension of the interlude with Trenton created a weird reaction in me, standing there in front of the open oven door, I was freezing cold.

It was as if I had been boxing and I had been successful at avoiding my opponent for most of the fight with my fancy footwork but he caught me off beat and sucker punched me. He'd hit me right in the stomach, sending me to double over in extreme pain. I fell to the floor in a wet rage, tears streaming down my face. Snot was oozing out of my nose.

I started to choke. I grabbed a tissue and walked back into the living room.

I cried out, "Why me?" Why do these things always happen to me? How did it turn out this way?

My breathing was staggered as I wept deeply out of despair. But I had done this to myself. There was no one to blame but me. I felt so stupid. He didn't love me; he couldn't possibly love me. If he loved me, I would not be left looking at the shattered images of my life, which seemed to be twirling about the living room like a carousel as a constant reminder of another decision gone badly. I wept loudly; so loud I felt the house shake all around me. I bowed my head in shame; I was a fool. I had been foolish enough to think that Trenton loved me and that a baby would make our relationship better.

I screamed silently. I screamed until I cried myself to sleep, right there on the living room floor beside the footprint Trenton's shoe left behind on the freshly vacuumed beige colored carpet, as he walked out on me.

Chapter 10

For though a righteous man falls seven times, he rises again, but the wicked are brought down by calamity.

Proverbs 24:16

It was 7:15 pm when he left and midnight when he came back. I was startled by the sound of keys clinging outside the front door. I quickly got my bearings together and scurried upstairs. I didn't want him to know that I cried myself to sleep in the shadow of his departure. The thought of him seeing me looking disheveled and feeling sorry for myself was not an option.

There I was pretending again. And for Trenton, why?

Once I got upstairs, I rushed into the bathroom to wipe the tearstains off my face. I barely turned on the water because he was inside the house. I heard him fidgeting around downstairs for about ten minutes before he climbed the stairs.

What was he doing?

My face was now washed and moisturized; I tiptoed into my bedroom and lay across the bed. I didn't want to chance it by trying to get under the covers, so I just made myself comfortable on top of them. By this point, I could hear him coming up the steps.

I shut my eyes as tightly as I could. I had to pretend that I wasn't fazed by his sudden departure even though I was severely shaken.

He walked over to the bed quickly after he crossed the threshold and peered down to see if I was awake. With my eyes still tightly shut, I relaxed a little and let out a deep breath and turned over. As I turned over, I felt his hand on my side. He nudged me slightly.

"Are you up?" He whispered.

I could smell the scotch on his breath. He had the nerve to go have drinks while I was here lamenting alone over our problem? I said nothing; I lay completely still. I didn't even allow my eyelids to flutter.

He kissed my cheek softly; his rough lips cut my skin just a little. The spicy smell of his liquor-laced breath caused my nose to wriggle. I opened my eyes and squinted, acting as if I had been sleeping soundly all along. "Hey," I said, in a raspy tone.

"Hey," he motioned for me to move over so that he could sit on the bed next to me. I scooted over.

"Did you just get here?" I played like I didn't know the answer.

"Yeah, I went out to think and had a drink. Afterwards I took a long drive."

So he had been drinking and driving. Great. "I'm glad you made it back all right. You've been drinking and driving? That probably wasn't the best thing to do."

"It was one drink." He hurled at me, slightly slurred.

It was clearly more than one drink.

"And?" I insisted.

"And what?" He sneered at me.

"Look, Trenton. I planned this romantic evening for us to share the most amazing news ever and you got up and walked out on me. Please don't come up in here playing with my feelings and acting as if nothing ever happened." I was sitting straight up now and I could feel my neck moving as I spoke emphatically.

"I'm sorry. I was just hoping that I could come back and we could get a good night's sleep and talk tomorrow."

"No, you weren't. You have known me long enough to know that I most definitely do not go to bed with matters unresolved and I know good and well you don't think it's cool that you got up and walked out of my house without acknowledging what I told you. I'm sorry to say that there is no way that we are sleeping together in this bed without talking *this* night." My voice started to rise and I did my best to bring it back down but whenever I got excited, anxious or upset, my voice started to rise and oftentimes it ended up so high pitched and loud that it was unrecognizable to the human ear.

"I spent the last four and a half hours trying to figure out how this happened."

"Oh, you know how this happened. Don't play coy now."

"You know what I mean, you are on the pill." He rolled his eyes at me.

"The only full-proof way to avoid pregnancy is to abstain and since we have been doing it like jack rabbits, I think it is safe to say that we haven't abstained and you know good and well that the possibility did exist." I couldn't let him know that I stopped taking my pills by mistake at first and then on purpose.

"I must be honest; I am not ready for this."

"And," I prodded.

"And, I am not ready for this." He repeated firmly.

"What does that mean, Trenton?" Now, I was getting agitated. What was I supposed to say to his comment? How was I supposed to respond? I was confused.

"It means that I don't think this is a good idea, we are just starting to get to know one another and I am not ready to be a parent. I don't see a child in my immediate future and I just don't know what else to say."

He looked at me with confusion in his eyes and then he added "I am not ready for this. I am sorry, but I am not."

"There is no "I" in us. I think that is part of your problem." I crossed my arms to illustrate my discomfort with his comment.

You could hear a pin drop. I took a deep breath and braced myself to ask the dreaded question.

"Does that mean you don't want the baby?"

"Yes, I don't want the baby."

"Wow. I can't believe that I am hearing this. I am good enough to lie up with but when it's time to pay, you want no parts of this? Wow."

"It's not like that; you make it sound so harsh and cruel."

"I make it sound like it is. You are telling me that this wasn't in the plan. Do you think it was in my plan? I love you and I thought that you loved me and wanted a future with me. Now I see that I was wrong."

"I do want a future with you, but I want to see what the future holds for us. It is too soon to be thinking about a baby. We haven't known each other that long. I believe that if we have a baby now, there will be no future for us."

"No, the time is now. Regardless of how long we've known each other, there is a baby now involved. We can't be selfish."

"Clearly you feel one way and I feel another," he dismissed my comment and turned away from me. "I can't help the way that I feel. I am not ready. I cannot tell you what to do because it is your body but I don't want a baby right now. I think that you having this baby would be a big mistake."

"So then our relationship is over?" I asked, trying to recover from the feeling of having swallowed my tongue.

"No, it's not over. I don't want it to be over. I am just stating my position. I want us to have a chance to grow together. We will be rushing into a place that we are not ready for if we have a baby right now. I think that if you want us to work, you need to think rationally. If you do, you will realize that I am right and now is not the time."

"But if I decide to keep the baby?"

"Be real, you know this is a bad idea too."

He never answered my question. I didn't know what to say. I was speechless. I was so confused; I had completely misjudged our relationship. I thought he loved me. He had said it so many times. I shook my head and tried to hold back the tears that were swelling my eyes.

Now, I felt like those words were just what I needed to hear to allow myself once again, to give in and fall into the bed with a man. I realize now that I was making the same mistake with a different man. I was so tired of falling into this trap.

When would I learn?

I so desperately needed to be loved that I would take whatever I could get. I hated that about me. I wasn't going to do this again. I needed space. I needed to think about how I was going to get myself out of this monster that I created.

"I must tell you, I am extremely confused. I don't know why this is happening to me. I have no idea how we got to this place." I paused and took a deep breath. "I need to think and I need to do it alone." I got up to walk him downstairs. I had to motion for him to follow me. "I will talk to you later."

He leaned in to kiss me; I pulled back and closed the door as he mouthed "sorry."

Yeah right, he wasn't sorry. At least that was how I felt at that time. I meandered back up the steps, sobbing incessantly. Every time I thought I was all cried out, I got my second wind and started again. Just remembering his face when he took the lid off that small brown box pierced my soul. I cringed at the sight of reliving seeing his beautiful smile go limp. It killed me. The memory of it had me feeling on edge. Not that I would ever actually harm myself, but I just couldn't take the scene of what just happened. It was too much for my weak heart.

I had finally gotten to a place where I was feeling complete. I felt like the part of my life that I had always been missing showed up when I fell for Trenton. He completed the puzzle. He had the good family background. He was kind and considerate. He was thoughtful and affectionate. He paid attention to me. He made me feel like I was enough. He made me feel like I had finally gotten to a place in my life where I deserved to be loved. Now I felt like the rug was being pulled out from under me. He said he wanted a family. Maybe Trenton didn't want one with me.

What did this mean for us? How would this turn out? I questioned myself.

I think part of the problem was that I "fell" for him. We should never "fall" for anything. We must do things with full knowledge and disclosure. Love should make us rise, not fall.

Emotional acts always get me into trouble; I scolded myself.

The thought of him saying that he didn't want our baby really let all the wind out of my sail. I felt like I had come so close but when I finally got there, I realized that I was in the wrong place. I was so lost. And what's worst is that I had no idea how to find my way back to safety.

I couldn't talk to God because I was a sinner, or at least that is what I told myself. I honestly felt like He would not honor my prayer because I was not living so that He would be pleased. I was so embarrassed; even too embarrassed to let God console me.

How did I get here? I had been so happy hours ago. I just knew that this was going to be the beginning of an amazing life with Trenton and our family.

I couldn't think about what to do now.

See, that's why you should have stuck to your guns and kept your beliefs in tact. Children are for marriage. The voice besieged me.

I didn't know how I was going to come out of this one on top. It was going to be a long night. There was no way that I could even think of sleeping but that is what I needed to do. The next day at work, I had an important presentation and there was no way that I could call out because it was my project and there was no one else working on it with me.

I took a deep breath as I crashed on my bed. I fixed my mind on my problem and started to ponder and the next thing I knew, my alarm was going off. I awoke grateful for a good night's sleep.

Chapter 11

Humble yourselves, therefore, under God's mighty hand, that he may lift you up in due time. Cast all your anxiety on him because he cares for you.

I Peter 5: 6, 7

The next morning at work went by in a blur. I was in and out of meetings all morning. My secretary left a few messages on my desk that Trenton had called. It wasn't that I was avoiding him on purpose, but it served him right to think so. I told myself that I would call him later but truthfully, I did not want to talk to Trenton at that time. I was so beside myself with work that I wasn't even able to focus any attention on my problems.

I just knew that he would love the idea of a little piece of us coming into this world. No doubt, having a baby was not going to be easy. Nothing that we want ever is, but I just knew he would be there with me throughout the entire process.

I was so mad at myself that I was falling into a depression. I had no idea what to do. My temperament had always been unstable when I felt neglected. This situation took me back to times when as a child, I had been neglected or abandoned by my mother or father. The results of the thought about those experiences were always the same, I wanted to curl up in the fetal position and stay there. I wanted to be left alone when I got the melancholies because I knew that any person within a one-foot radius of me had the potential to get caught in my crossfire.

I was jolted back to reality by a reminder on my online calendar that I needed to call another department about my project design. I had to snap out of it. I had to re-channel my energy. I was going to have to do what I did best, fake it. I was the queen of letting no one see me sweat. I could hide the truth from the best of them. My emotions and feelings oftentimes took a back seat to my ambition or my desire to let no one in on what I was dealing with.

I thought I wanted a baby so bad and especially a baby with Trenton. But, I also could not see myself as a single mother. I never wanted to be a single mother. I had tried so hard up to this point in life to prevent myself from being affiliated with any stereotypes. If I had this baby without Trenton being an active participant, in my mind I would become a statistic.

You will be a statistic no matter which way it goes, stupid. You will be a single mother, just what you always tried to avoid. Look what you've done. That's what you get for trying to force a man to love you. You are not lovable. The voice beleaguered me.

You've gone and become just what you said you never would.

I really struggled with the thoughts filling my mind. Not that I was expecting Trenton to marry me just because I had gotten pregnant, but I thought that we were on the same page about the future.

I needed someone to talk to who would provide an unbiased opinion. I hadn't told anyone that I was pregnant. I guess I wanted Trenton to be the first person that knew of our pending arrival.

And I remembered that they say that you don't tell people until your second trimester. As a result, I wasn't planning on spilling the beans any time soon. I always felt bad for those people who told everyone as soon as they took the test and then suffered a miscarriage.

And now that things were not looking positive, I definitely was glad that I hadn't opened my mouth. I hadn't even told my mother, and by this time, we had a real good relationship. I couldn't talk to my friends about this just yet but I felt a strong desire to reach out to a close associate at work. I knew in my heart she would advise me well.

Shiloh and I had gotten close over the years at the firm. I felt very comfortable seeking her opinion on matters because she was down to earth and had a personal relationship with God but didn't act "holier than thou." She never judged me for the decisions I made about anything that I felt I was big and bad enough to do. She would always challenge me and help me to see the error of my ways without pointing it out and making me feel stupid. Shiloh had a slow and steady manner that allowed her to evaluate a situation, pray about it and then respond.

I took a deep breath and picked up my phone. I dialed her extension.

"Hey Shiloh, did I catch you at a bad time? You got a quick minute?"

"Hey girl, what's up?" I definitely considered Shiloh a friend.

"Do you have lunch plans?"

"No, what's going on?"

"Can we meet for lunch? I need to get your opinion on something."

"Sure, what time do you want to meet?" Shiloh was smiling through the phone. I glanced down at my watch. It was eleven-thirty.

"How's noon? I have a 1:15 pm meeting. I would love to go out and enjoy some of this beautiful fall day. We can go to *Deep Blue*, my treat. Okay?" I talked fast and barely gave her a chance to understand me, let alone voice any concerns or opinions.

"Yeah, okay," she paused. "I'll see you then." She hung up.

I took another deep breath because half the battle was over.

My phone rang; it was Shiloh. "Hey."

"Hey, sorry you don't sound well. Is everything okay? I know I'm going to see you in a few minutes but I just wanted to give you a quick call back to let you know that I am here for you and I know that something's not right. I said a little prayer as we hung up before and the spirit told me to call you back."

"I appreciate that Shiloh. We will talk in a bit but I am managing. I have a few calls to return since I was in meetings all morning. I'll see you in a few." I smiled as I hung up the phone.

I was glad that I had Shiloh to lean on at this time. I really loved that she was a little older and married and settled into her life. I loved that she was a Christian and she would pray with me and help to increase my confidence and faith. I was so glad that she was placed in my life. We worked together on the same team a few years back and just kept our relationship going as we moved on to new positions.

I took another deep breath and gathered my thoughts. This was going to be a trying hour. I returned a few calls quickly. As I hung up the phone, my line lit up with Trenton's cell phone number. I sent him to voicemail. I wasn't ready to talk with him yet. I really wanted to let him stew in his own confusion.

Another peek at my watch revealed that it was five of twelve. I got my wallet and sunglasses and walked to the overpass to meet Shiloh.

I pasted on my pretentious smile as I got on the elevator and took it down to the second floor. *Never let them see you sweat.* I must have gotten on the local instead of the express because we stopped on every floor.

"Ah, lunch time," I said out loud. Finally, we were on the 2nd floor.

Okay, girl. Get it together, I thought to myself as I looked up to see Shiloh's smiling face walking towards me. She was waving vigorously. I could tell she was happy to see me.

"Hey there," she smiled at me while reaching out to give me a hug. Shiloh was beautiful; she had an uncanny resemblance to Courtney Cox except she was a blonde.

That hug felt so good. It took everything in me not to break down and cry right then and there. It was so nice to feel a set of welcoming arms around me. I could tell immediately that she genuinely cared for me.

"Hey," I managed to get out; I must admit I did get a little choked up.

"So how's your day going so far?" Shiloh asked, getting in step beside me, matching stride for stride.

"Ugh, it is a busy time right now. I feel like the reports and meetings just don't stop. I was in meetings all morning and I have two more when I get back from lunch. Days like this make it hard to stay on track with my to-do list. You know, they want to meet about everything. Anyway, I'm babbling. It's all good, I guess I shouldn't complain."

"Oh, it's okay, we are busy too. I think that in my department, no one wants to meet about anything. So it's just every man for him or herself. I am so tired. The boys have been sick and Rob has been working doubles at the hospital the past few nights. So, you know what that means, Mommy doesn't sleep." Shiloh took a deep breath. I could tell how tired she was. It made my heart hurt.

"Oh, Shiloh, I'm sorry. Here I am burdening you with my problems and you are sleep-deprived. I am being so selfish." I lamented. Now, I really felt bad.

"No, don't you dare feel bad," she said as if she was reading my mind. "I am here to help; I am not doing God's will if I am selfish. It is my job to be selfless. Don't mention it. I know you'd do the same for me," she finished as she patted me on the back.

"You always have a way of making me feel like part of the family." I turned to face her, forcing her to stop dead in her tracks. "Thank you, I truly appreciate you being here for me."

Again, I almost lost it.

By the time she hugged me again, we were just about at *Deep Blue*, a local seafood restaurant with a lunch buffet. You could get lump crab cakes and crab legs on the buffet and everything tasted so amazing. I didn't have much of an appetite but the atmosphere was warm and welcoming, which was just what the doctor ordered.

"Two please," Shiloh told the hostess. The hostess smiled; and proceeded to show us to our seats. That was the other thing I loved about *Deep Blue*, there was never a wait.

"Sheila will be your waitress and she will be over in a minute to take your order, may I start you ladies off with something to drink?"

"I'll have water with no lemon. I'm going to have the buffet."

"I'll have unsweetened iced tea and I also would like to have the buffet." Shiloh smiled at the hostess. She looked in my direction as the waitress walked away.

I looked up at her and smiled, and then I waited for her to get out of earshot so that I could fill Shiloh in. I took a deep breath and braced myself. I wasn't really sure how to say it; but I figured I better come up with something.

Chapter 12

In the same way, the Spirit helps us in our weakness. We do not know what we ought to pray for, but the Spirit himself intercedes for us with groans that words cannot express.

Romans 8:26

"Okay, I asked you here today so that I could talk to you and get your opinion on my current situation. I value your opinion and I knew that in talking with you, you wouldn't stand in judgment of me as I tell you what's going on." I looked up at her; my head had been bowed in shame as I talked. I was truly embarrassed about my choices and what I did to get to where I am.

"Hey, look at me."

I raised my head.

"I am here for you. Don't feel like you have to be anyone other than you."

"Thanks, I needed that. Okay, here it goes. I am pregnant. I just found out and I was so excited that Trenton and I were having a baby. I prepared this special dinner and everything and I got him a present, a silver rattle, and when he opened it, instead of being excited like me he turned and walked out on me and didn't come back for five hours." I breathed. I had to get it all out before I lost my nerve.

"I'm sorry, what?" Shiloh looked at me kind of bewildered, like she was a deer caught in my headlights.

I giggled; talking too fast was always a problem for me and once I got excited, you could forget it. I repeated myself, slower the second time. I took a deep breath when I was finished.

"Wow." Shiloh wiped her brow.

I could tell that she didn't know what to say.

"I know I just laid a lot on you. But I am scared and I need guidance. When Trenton did come back, all he kept saying was that 'he wasn't ready for this.' He made it clear that he did not want the baby. I don't know what to do. I was led to talk to you about this. I didn't know who else to talk to."

Shiloh stood out in my mind immediately as I thought about who I would confide in. I didn't have to be anyone but myself when it came to her. She was true and genuine and I knew that my secret, shame and guilt would all be safe with her.

"Did you talk to God?"

I looked at her; my eyes got so big. I wasn't expecting that. "I'm sorry, what?" I said and chuckled nervously.

Had I talked to God about my sin? No, definitely not. Truthfully, I hadn't even thought about it, what I would say; I created this monster.

I shook my head "no." Instantly I felt embarrassed.

"Well, the first thing we need to do is pray." Shiloh said confidently in a tone low enough for only me to hear.

"Okay." I bowed my head to pray with Shiloh. I have to admit I wasn't focused. I lifted my head slightly and peeked out of the corner of my eye to see what was going on around us.

I was so afraid that people would be looking at us and wondering what was going on. I was so tense; I couldn't let my guard down.

She grabbed my hands. I looked up, startled. I thought maybe she knew that I was a little uneasy about this public prayer. But if she knew, she didn't let on.

She said, "Holding hands helps to establish God's Word. When two people stand together in agreement in Jesus' name, He comes and stands with them, and we need His presence right now."

"Amen," I gave her a nervous smile.

Shiloh began the prayer, "Dear Lord, we come to You in the name of our Lord and Savior, Jesus Christ. We ask that You give us peace and help us to live in a manner that makes You pleased with us. We ask that You forgive us for our actions that were not pleasing in Your sight, those things done knowingly and unknowingly. Lord, I pray that You give peace and strength to my dear friend right now, in the name of Jesus. Stand in the gap and fill her with Your love and spirit, dear Lord. Guide her so that she will know what steps to take and what to do in this and all situations. Most importantly, Lord please illustrate to her that You love her. Show her that Your love and acceptance is all she really needs. Thank You for allowing me to intercede on her behalf. We thank You for these and all blessings. I pray this prayer in Jesus' name, amen."

"Amen." I was impressed. Shiloh sounded like she knew what she was talking about. I knew I had made the right choice about who to talk to.

My friends would be focusing on what Trenton did and not helping me to figure out what to do. Or, they would be talking me into something that I wasn't entirely sure about. Plus, I was so embarrassed by my choices that I didn't want to deal with criticism and backlash from others.

I needed someone who would be there to help me. I had a feeling that Shiloh would be, without judging me.

"Shiloh, I have to be honest, I am not interested in being a single mother. I can't do this alone. No, change that. I don't want to do this alone. Not that I can't, but I don't want to. I saw this as an opportunity to begin the process of making things right with my life. I felt that having a child now would help me to undo the wrong done to me by my parents. It is up to me to be better than my family situation and if I become a single parent by making a poor choice, I have recreated the wheel. I can't do that." One tear from each eye rolled down my cheeks.

"Okay. Well, let me ask you a question. If that is the case and you don't want to be a single mother, why did you let this happen? You and Trenton are not married and may not become married just because you are pregnant, which means that if you did have the child, you would be a single mother."

Ouch. I was kind of stunned. I think she could sense my discomfort.

But Shiloh was right.

"I'm sorry but I have to ask you these questions. Part of the problem is that you lack guidance and you are making decisions for other people without any consideration for them. You are being selfish. So, excuse me for my directness, but why did you let this happen?"

I looked her right in the face and I withheld the whole truth.

"It was an accident. I am on the pill. I missed a few pills. I didn't expect this to happen."

Instantly, I felt so bad. Here I was asking Shiloh to help me, we just prayed to God and I didn't tell her the complete truth. I did not have a sincere heart and somehow I knew that God did not like how I responded.

But what could I do? I was waist deep in my mess by now. There wasn't a life jacket or shovel anywhere in sight.

But I couldn't tell her the whole truth. I was so stupid and used poor judgment and I didn't want anyone to know what I had done. No one could know that I had created this monster. I had to keep that to myself.

"Okay, so mistakes happen. If you weren't planning it, you can understand Trenton's resistance to the idea. I don't know Trenton but maybe he will come around."

I shook my head.

"Shiloh, you weren't there. I don't know if I believe that. Besides, what if he doesn't? I cannot be a single mother. I don't want to be one of those women having to chase the father to get child support because he wants nothing to do with the child."

"Well, let me be clear. Regardless of how things play out, if you have a baby in nine months, you will be a single mother. Even if you have the baby and Trenton helps you everyday, if you are not married, you are considered single and therefore, you will be a single mother. Sorry to say it but you will be a single mother." She really drove the point home.

Again, I felt stupid. Shiloh was right. I hadn't thought things through.

"You are right. This is bad. I am in a bad place and I don't know what to do. The man I love doesn't want our baby. I don't want to have a "baby's daddy." I was laughing but on the verge of crying at the same time.

What had I done? I am so stupid. In my twisted logic I thought that I would be able to pull this off. It all seemed like such a golden plan.

She shook her head. "First of all, you make it sound like it is a bad thing. Second of all, do you really think Trenton will be that way? If you do, then you shouldn't be with him anyway. Confusion and denial are normal symptoms in this situation. He is not acting atypical. But if he cares for you at all, which he must, he will understand if you decide to keep the baby."

"But I don't want to make the decision myself. I am not strong enough."

"Well," Shiloh said. "If Trenton is clearly telling you that he doesn't want a baby now, you are making the decision yourself. What do *you* want?"

"I don't know. I have been turning the idea around in my head since he walked out on me the other night and I just don't know what I want. All I do know is that I don't know what to do. He claimed that he loved me yet, when the chips were down and it was time for us to come together, he walked out on me. He left me hanging. I don't know how I feel about that. I mean he came back saying it wasn't over and all but I don't know. To be honest, I am really starting to feel uncomfortable with being pregnant and he clearly doesn't want it."

By now, the tears were welling up in the corners of my eyes. One got away and traveled the lonely road down my cheek.

"Shiloh, I can't do this by myself. I am not strong enough. I can't do this. If he doesn't want it, I can't do this by myself." I pleaded.

"But you won't be alone. You'll have your family and close friends, you'll have me."

At that, I started laughing. It was a nervous laugh. I had to make my point.

"Are you kidding? I can't count on my family. Right now, I feel like an island. And my friends, no one even knows that I am pregnant. They have their own issues. They may be excited at first, but eventually, they will leave me too. Sure, there would be a baby shower and visits at the hospital after the birth but eventually I will be alone. I just can't do this by myself. I am the one that everyone thinks has it together. I am the one who is always telling everyone how I am going to conquer the world. I can't see that happening with a baby on my hip."

Boy, I had been stupid. What love makes us do; I was embarrassed by my actions.

"Okay, calm down. Promise me that you will take your time and think about it. Don't make any rush decisions. Give Trenton a chance to calm down and think things through. In the meantime, check out all of your options. But no matter what, make sure that you are okay with whatever decision you choose. And also, make the decision for you, not Trenton."

Make the decision for me, not Trenton. What did that mean?

I played the role of being strong and confident but I was really a very timid person with low self-esteem. My own shadow scared me. The thought of actually becoming as great as I pretended I was frightened me beyond normal belief. I felt like Trenton was my ticket out of the hell in which I lived. If he didn't want this baby and I had it, he would leave me and I would have to fend for myself. I wasn't up for that.

I had always allowed myself to get sucked in by the men in my life. I had always placed their importance over that of my own and allowed their needs to take precedence. I blamed my dad for that. Being a little girl who wasn't loved the right way makes it hard to differentiate between the right way and the wrong way to be loved and to love someone. But because he never told me he loved me, I desperately sought out the wrong types of relationships with men. I had a "take what you can get" mentality rather than a "price above rubies" reality. I accepted enough rather than realizing that I deserved more than enough. I got caught up. My need for love jacked me up, big time.

In my haste and need for love I became blind to their issues and pretended like I didn't see the truth. I was so use to settling that it became a part of the natural composition of my life.

My relationship with Trenton proved to be no different. I was trying to rationalize staying with a man who clearly did not place enough value on my jewels. Here he was treating me like a cubic zirconia rather than a diamond. And I was letting him. I had been so foolish. I convinced myself that since a diamond and cubic zirconia looked just alike and the human eye couldn't tell the difference, it was okay to defraud myself. But it wasn't okay. To the naked eye, they looked exactly the same, but when put under the light, the truth comes out. A cubic zirconia can't hold a candle to a diamond.

Now, if I could only make myself believe that I was a diamond.

All I could see was that this was somehow my fault. Because I had jumped the gun and gotten pregnant, I now had to pay the consequences. I wanted us to have a baby. I wanted us to be a family. I saw my future with Trenton; but, if he was rejecting our child, didn't that mean that he was rejecting me?

I looked at my watch and realized I needed to get back for my meeting. I hadn't even touched my food.

Shiloh was looking at me and her lips were moving. She had been talking the whole time but I was in a committed personal conversation. I had been lost in thought and contemplating my future while she was talking.

"I'm sorry, Shiloh. You were saying something but I was in another world." She smiled at my face of confusion. I could feel the love radiating from her.

"Oh, it's okay. I know you have a lot on your mind. I just want you to know that I am here for you anytime you need to talk. I want you to search your heart. Give yourself some space. Trenton will be there when you are ready to talk but don't rush into anything. Take a few days and think. Weigh the pros and cons. What will your life be like with the baby and without the baby? Then ask yourself the same question but substitute Trenton. I know you don't want to think of your life without Trenton, but this could be the end of your relationship if you can't see eye to eye. And I am here to tell you that it won't be the end of the world if you move on. I am not trying to scare you or point you in any direction but I really just want you to think. Promise me that you will take the time to think."

I nodded at her. "I will. I promise."

Just then our server appeared with the check. Shiloh paused although she looked as if she was about to say something else. I grabbed my wallet and pulled out my debit card. Sheila walked out briskly promising a prompt return. Sheila was back with my copy to sign; I quickly scribbled my name and we were out the door.

"Shiloh, you were saying. Sorry I had to cut you off. Because it is almost one and I have that 1:15 pm meeting, I needed to get that check handled."

"No problem, I just want you to really consider your options. And remember that God does not make mistakes. If he brings you to it; he will bring you through it."

That was so true. I had a lot to think about.

"Thank you Shiloh. I appreciate you so much and thank you for praying with me. Thank you for even taking time away from your day to meet with me and help me to sort through this. Because of you, I have some great advice to ponder and I know that you have helped me more than I can thank you for." I gave her a deep hug.

We walked the rest of the way back to the firm in silence. I was thinking about everything that Shiloh said and Shiloh, she was taking in the beautiful September day. I could see her smile out of the corner of my eye and I could tell that she was happy to be having some adult conversation after a few nights of dealing with her sons alone while her husband pulled doubles at the hospital.

We got back to the building in no time. Shiloh reached in and gave me another hug and I hugged her back tightly. We parted and I returned down the long corridor toward my department. I had to hustle to make it back to my desk and grab my notebook because the meeting would start in about ten minutes. The baby and Trenton were going to have to take a back seat, for now.

By the time I had gotten off of work, Trenton had called me ten more times. I thought about what Shiloh said; then, I turned off my cell phone.

I still wasn't sure what I wanted to do and I didn't want to be confused or talked into or out of anything until I knew how I wanted to handle the situation. I have to admit, I was confused; yet, I kept going back to Shiloh's prayer at lunch.

She prayed that God would grant me strength. That was what confused me. I felt weak. I felt helpless. I felt like a baby bird that had fallen from the nest before my wings were fully developed. I was down on the ground but no one was coming to save me and take me back to security in the nest. My mother and father were gone. I had no idea what to do. The way things looked, no matter what I decided, I was up for a struggle. I wasn't ready to do this myself. That was for sure. I wasn't prepared to give up Trenton. That was for sure. If I kept the baby, he would leave me. If I didn't have the baby, I would resent him. There was no way to win. Or was there?

Chapter 13

Create in me a pure heart, O God, and renew a steadfast spirit within me.

Psalm 51:10

The scent of ammonia mixed with hydrangea was the first thing that greeted me when my eyes opened. I blinked about twenty times trying to get myself to focus in on my surroundings. I looked around the room and tried to get my bearings. I felt tight around my wrists and my throat was dry. My position was extremely uncomfortable. The room was closing in on me. I felt hot and my air passages appeared to be blocked as I tried to focus on the blurry objects around me.

As I desperately tried to regain my focus, I started to sweat massively. I couldn't focus in and it was causing me to panic. My breathing deepened as I began to feel like my next breath was not certain.

All I could see were blurred images behind the gray curtain that separated me from my growing sin. The figures moved back and forth almost methodically tending to the concerns of my fellow roommates. I blinked my eyes profusely as I was still not quite sure of my location and what exactly had happened. I focused in on the clock and blinked again attempting to get the clock face to be focused in so that I would be able to see the time.

When I was finally able to see clearly, it was 10:30. I had been out the entire time; I didn't remember a thing. I felt a little cramping but for the most part I was just tired and groggy. I felt the need to sleep. It was an unwelcome slumber, as if someone had personally come and put their fingers on my eyelids and ushered me into another dimension. I was fighting it because I wanted to be alert to find out what was happening around me. I felt a tingling feeling pulsing throughout my body.

As I surveyed the room, I could feel the walls closing in on me. I broke out in a cold sweat and my heart started beating five times faster than normal. I couldn't breathe. I tried to speak to let someone know I needed help but couldn't fix my lips to make a sound. All of sudden everything around me went black.

There was a bright light welcoming me and it felt gentle and painless so I moved toward it with a bright smile on my face. Suddenly, the bright light disappeared and I was left with a gray and dull feeling surrounding me. I tried to get up; I couldn't. I felt like I was floating. I couldn't understand what was happening; I had passed out. I had suffered a reaction to coming off of the general anesthesia.

While I was blacked out, I replayed what led up to me lying in this recovery room bed. Tears flowed freely down my face as I looked back over what I had done. I had done something terrible. I felt my pulse tighten again as I searched for a breath to eradicate my current state. I couldn't find one; I was stuck in the aftermath of the mess that I had made. How did I get here? How did this happen? Why was I so fixed on trying to trap him and increase the pressure of our relationship?

I felt more warm tears fall on my face, which was cold like the rest of my body as a result of my incessant shivering. I grabbed a blanket and tried to warm myself to no avail.

I decided not to have the baby. It was a tumultuous decision. It was admittedly one of the hardest decisions I have ever made in my life. But I couldn't do it. I couldn't go through with ruining a child's life because I wanted to have life my way. Trenton kept calling throughout those two weeks and leaving messages stating he wanted us to have a future and we could have a baby later. He kept telling me that we needed to take some time and allow us to develop as a couple.

"If we had a baby now," he said, "we would ruin it."

The thought of ruining another life really impacted me into deciding that a baby now might not be a good idea. I guess that's why the Bible says, "Thou shalt not covet." As we've all heard before, what's good for the goose is not good for the gander. The baby enhanced the life of my friend. The thought of having this baby was killing me softly, in more ways than one.

He claimed to be thinking in our best interest because he knew that I was emotionally involved and couldn't think straight.

Was he calling me stupid?

I would replay his messages and just think about what he said. Part of me knew that being a single mother was not an option and the other part of me agreed with what he said.

What did that say about me?

I'd watched countless friends and family members struggle to make ends meet because of the deadbeat dads that promised they would be there. Trenton was telling me plain and simple that he would not commit to being a part of the child's life.

How could I stay with him?

I was afraid of bringing a child into this world and not being able to protect her from what I dealt with as a child. And if Trenton didn't want the baby, that meant he wouldn't be able to protect her either. I kept going back over what happened to me as a child in my mind. I kept thinking about how my parents hadn't protected me or prevented my innocence from being stolen.

I just knew my luck and because of it, I would have a daughter that someone else would molest because I wouldn't be strong enough to prevent it.

The past was my curse, I said vehemently to myself.

I kept thinking that maybe he would change his mind, but I couldn't bank on that. I had to act as if he meant what he said from the very beginning.

I told myself lots of lies to make excuses for the choice I was making. I couldn't do that to a child. There was no guarantee that we would be a family unit if I had a child now without the papers. If I wasn't married to Trenton there was nothing to keep him from moving on to the next woman. I had convinced myself that there was no way that I could bring a child into that confusion.

I was protecting her from my past.... the mess, the sorrow and from the shame that I felt was my life. If I could turn back time, I would have been more rational and thought through my choices when I missed those two pills.

If I had thought things through, I wouldn't be in this mess. More importantly, I wouldn't be a murderer.

The way I saw it, we could have a baby later but I felt at that time I was way too weak to live without Trenton. Don't ask me why I felt that way, but I did. I honestly did not feel that I wanted to be without him. He had become my life and I allowed myself to get lost in him. I loved his family.

With all that I had been through with my own family, I needed the security of Trenton's.

Besides, it had been my bright idea to create this entire problem. If I didn't take matters into my own hand, we would be happy. Wouldn't we?

It was my fault and since I made a mistake, I had to correct it.

I poured these lies into my mind to make it okay. I had to dowse the flames of my burning sin.

During the two weeks without communication with Trenton, I felt like a junkie going through the detoxification process. My time apart from him was complete with the shakes and nights filled with cold sweats. He continued to call everyday. I realized that being without him was not an option. I missed his voice. I missed his presence. I missed his smile.

Each call said the same thing. "Hey, baby. How are you? I miss you. I hope that you are okay. I hope you realize that I do love you. It may not seem like it right now, but I do. I am working everyday to secure our future so that we can have a family but now is not the time. I am thinking about us, you are not thinking clearly. Call me, please. I need to hear from you. I need to hear your voice."

I would cry after each voicemail. This was by far the hardest thing for me to do.

How could this be happening?

Once I made the decision, I had to act on it and fast. I knew myself and if I sat on it too long, I would talk myself out of it. I knew this had to be done. I had scheduled the procedure for the next day. I had already checked with my insurance and they would pay for it. I hadn't told Trenton.

My initial plan was just to have the procedure and then say I lost the child. But then I decided that I did not want to go that route. I had to tell him because I needed someone to drive me. Because of the anesthesia, I couldn't drive. I hadn't told anyone other than Shiloh that I was even pregnant so I definitely couldn't expect anyone else to take me to the clinic. I took a deep breath and picked up my phone.

I dialed his number.

He answered on the first ring. "Hello," he said kind of hurried. He caught his breath. "Hey, how are you?"

"I am fine." I was short and to the point.

I had an attitude as soon as I heard his voice. I was so upset at myself and even at Trenton that this was even happening. "I'm going to the clinic tomorrow. I need a ride. Are you free?"

"You are doing what?" He sounded surprised.

"I am aborting your child. It's tomorrow. I need a ride."

I said each word slow and exaggerated. I had hoped that hearing me say "his child" would make him rethink his initial stance on the issue. I had been so wrong.

"Okay, whatever you need. Are you sure this is what you want?"

"It's what I have to do. Can you pick me up at 7 am? I need to be there by 7:30 and my appointment is at 9 am. There's preparation and blood work that has to be done when I arrive."

"And you are sure about this?" Trenton asked again.

I took a deep breath. I couldn't deal with this. "Have you changed your mind? Do you want the baby?"

"No, I haven't. I do not want the baby."

My heart sank again. I thought that maybe just maybe after two weeks without me he might have changed his mind.

"Well then. I'll see you in the morning."

"Baby..."

I hung up. I took a deep breath. I got down on my knees and I prayed that God would forgive me for what I was about to do.

"Dear Lord," I said. "It's me again. I am here to ask for Your forgiveness in advance for the serious sin that I am about to commit. Lord, I am going to have an abortion. I know that You probably don't view this as a mistake but I do. I made a big mistake and I can't do this. I am not strong enough to be a single mother. I need to know that You will allow me to do this but that I will still be able to have a family some day. I am so young and so screwed up from what my family did to me that I was foolish enough to believe that maybe, just maybe, this would fix me. I see now that I was wrong. I wish that I never did any of it. But I pray that You will have mercy on me, anyway. God please help me. I don't know why I keep messing up. I don't know why I keep trying to fix my life myself. I pray this prayer in Jesus' name, Amen."

I got up and staggered to my bed. I cried myself to sleep. I was really depressed. I had done this for love. This was the love that was supposed to take me to my next level. Love clearly wasn't all that it was cracked up to be.

I awoke the next morning to the sound of a horn blaring out front. As I looked out the window, it appeared that a neighbor was getting a ride to work. It was six am. I got up and jumped in the shower so that I would be ready when Trenton arrived.

Trenton was on time; I got into the car without even a hello. I was so upset. I needed to do this and get this behind us so we could move on. Would we be able to move on? I wasn't sure; but I would have to see if we had what it takes to make it last.

I got to the clinic and told him when to come back to get me. I prepared to go inside alone. As I started to open the door, he turned me to him and stared into my eyes.

"Can I wait for you inside? I would really like to be there with you."

"Why?"

"I don't know; I just feel the need to be with you."

"Well, it's too late for that. If you were with me, I wouldn't be here."

He was silent.

I shrugged my shoulders. "No, they have a strict policy." I lied. I was getting good at it, why stop now? I continued, "Only patients are allowed. I should be ready to leave around noon. I have to have a two-hour recovery period. Can you get here at 11:30 just to be safe? I don't want to have to wait for you and sit here longer. Okay? Thanks."

"Okay, I'll see you then." His tone was somber.

He leaned over to kiss me but I let myself out of the car. Right then, I didn't even want him to touch me.

I guess I had my own visions of what going to an abortion clinic would be like. I expected picketers on the driveway with big bright signs letting it be known that they were against abortion. I envisioned signs that read "Abortion = Murder." But no one was there. There was no hoopla whatsoever. I think that deep down part of me was disappointed. On television, they sensationalized the act of killing an unborn fetus. I guess I should have been happy that I didn't have any extra drama to contend with but I almost wanted someone to make me feel horrible about what I was doing. Surely, I had convinced myself that if someone else had an opinion, I would change my mind.

It was just a regular white building. In fact, the outside of the clinic looked like any other building. It could easily have been a real estate agency or some other business. I took a deep, long, freeing breath and prepared myself to enter the building.

As I opened the doors into the reception area, I saw the bright white walls. They were so bright it looked as if someone came along and painted them everyday. I could smell the antiseptic and *Pine Sol* mix, which disinfected the environment.

As I meandered up to the front desk to sign in, a young girl, maybe 15 or 16 caught my attention. She looked very sad. I could see the pain in her big gray eyes. The gray of her eyes had a bluish black tint to them, like that of a mood ring. I could tell she was being forced to have an abortion.

Her mother stood beside her with a stoic stance, her arms folded. I could see the angst running across her mother's jaw line. Her square chin spoke to me, saying that her daughter would ruin her life if she had a baby at this age and that she was doing this for her own good. She was too young to be a grandmother and she wanted her daughter to finish her education and change her destiny. If she had the baby, welfare would be her future.

I was there almost of my own free will. Yet, looking at her mother then back at the young girl, I wondered if this was for my own good.

I tried not to be too emotionally charged, as this was hard enough. If I got too focused on my feelings, I would be turning around and leaving. But since I was not sure if I was equipped to be a single mother, I had to do this. Although I hated Trenton right now, he was an important part of my life. I had truly convinced myself that I needed him to survive. He had a way of pouring into me the love that I had desired for so long in my life.

He wasn't perfect but he had always treated me good enough.

My standards were apparently very low, I thought as I reflected.

The receptionist greeted me, taking off some of the edge. She gave me a few forms to fill out and asked for my insurance card so that she could make a copy. I have to tell you honestly, the fact that my insurance was footing the bill made this decision a little bit easier. At this point in my life I was living "poor check to poor check" and extra money was not plentiful. And since Trenton was as broke as a joke, that definitely helped to lessen the blow.

I finished filling out my forms and returned to the receptionist. She smiled, gave them the once over, handed me back my insurance card and pointed to the waiting room. She told me to have a seat. It was about twenty minutes before I was ushered behind the door leading to the exam rooms. Once there, I began to get anxious and scared. I knew what I had to do but I hated the fact that I was doing it.

What had I done? I had ended the life that God had given me. I had chosen a man over my own child. I was no better than my mother, sisters, cousins and even some friends. All my life, I had witnessed one woman or another in my family choose a man over her children. I promised myself that I would never do the same thing; I promised my future children that I would be different. Yet, here I was, the same as those I had inwardly criticized for being so stupid.

Blood is thicker than water, I told myself. I had chosen water. Again, I asked myself, was it worth the trouble that I was now going through as a result of this poor choice?

Even in having an abortion, I had kept the generational curse going and perpetuated it one step further because I was weak and unable to stand on my own. I sought validation from a man and he told me to abort our child. I was a fool; and, it was too late.

I grabbed my purse and dug through all the clutter inside to find my mirrored compact. I looked at myself in the mirror. My espresso brown eyes stared back at me in a condescending manner.

You should have known better, they said to me. *How could you let a man come before your child? Don't you know that it is better to put your trust in God than to put your confidence in man*? My eyes chided me.

I felt a swift gush of guilty tears cover my face. I couldn't grab the tissues beside the recovery room bed fast enough. I cleared the tears, trying to wipe away the guilt that was now filling my lungs. I couldn't breathe. I gasped for air but came up short. I couldn't believe that the life God granted me was gone; it was a memory. I had killed someone.

You are a murderer; my eyes continued to scold me from the reflection in the mirror. Looking at the woman in the mirror scared me. It scarred me. I had put a man's life before that of my child. I was a murderer. I was a selfish, timid woman. I was my mother. I was my sister. I didn't know if I would ever forgive myself.

"Hello, there. Welcome back to us. Your procedure was uneventful; we did not run into any complications." The registered nurse who assisted the doctor stated as she opened the curtain to check on me.

"You will start to feel some discomfort and you will likely be sore for the next 48 hours. I hope you took a few days off from work to recuperate and I hope that you will have someone at home to assist you."

I grimaced at her; I hadn't thought of that.

She could sense my concern. "You should not do any heavy lifting for at least 4-5 days."

I hadn't slightly considered the fact that I might not be able to do the day to day things in life. The sight of Trenton still made me sick. And no one else knew I had been pregnant let alone that I had dissolved the pregnancy. I had no idea how I was going to convince someone to look after me for that amount of time.

I looked up to see the nurse's lips were still moving. She had been talking that whole time and I had been completely oblivious to what she was telling me.

"I'm sorry, I missed everything you said. I have been in another world. Can you repeat everything?" I felt so stupid, again.

"No problem, it is common to have a distracted spirit after coming out of the procedure. Just take a deep breath. It's the affects of the anesthesia."

I inhaled deeply; I could feel it down in my soul. I had a distracted spirit.

She proceeded to give me some recovery instructions.

"Wow, that's a lot. Is there anything else?" I was glad that everything she said was also in writing.

"No, that is about it but you may want to eat a very light diet. You will be able to leave here at noon. Do you need to call anyone for a ride?"

"No, my ride will be here waiting for me at 11:30. Thank you." I smiled dryly. My throat was still very dry. "May I have a glass of water?"

"My pleasure, now take this time to rest." With that, she was gone, behind the curtain.

I took her advice and closed my eyes. When I woke up again, it was time to get dressed and go home. I got dressed as fast as I could and went out to the lobby and signed myself out. As I requested, Trenton was sitting out front when I opened the double doors. I faked a smile in his direction as he got out to open my door for me.

"Hey," he said weakly. I could tell he didn't know what to say to me, which was great. I wanted him to say absolutely nothing.

Chapter 14

Now forgive my sin once more and pray to the Lord your God to take this deadly plague away from me.

Exodus 10:17

The weeks following the abortion were horrid. I was a basket case complete with menacing nightmares and thoughts of suicide. I had become an insomniac and fought urges to compare myself with other people I knew, leaving myself to feel completely out of place, an island and desperately insufficient. And when I woke myself up to escape the devastating blows I endured during my nightmares, I cried myself back to sleep. This story reran every night for weeks. The torrents of rain that were my tears stained several sets of bed sheets.

I couldn't stand the sight of myself in the mirror. My reflection made me vomit. I hated the person looking back at me, all over again. I hated that I had reduced my existence to this.

I couldn't believe that I had allowed Trenton to put me in this position. I hated myself for not being strong enough to stand up for what I wanted. I allowed him to control me like a puppeteer. It was sad to say, but he held the strings.

Moreover, the hardest part of this whole situation was that the only person I could share my pain with was Trenton and I wanted nothing to do with him. We were still together but we weren't. I couldn't get out of my funk. I needed help and I needed it bad. I didn't know where else to turn so I activated the personal assistance service available through work and scheduled a session with a therapist.

I thought that maybe if I talked to someone I didn't know, than she would be able to help me. Because no one knew that I was pregnant, I couldn't confide in anyone. I think that made it worse because I had no outlet. I truly was alone. All Trenton did was give me a headache. Whenever we would talk about the abortion, it turned into a fight because he was not sensitive to what I had gone through. It was easy for him to feel normal and want life to go on because he had not endured anything. He had not had surgery to remove something vital from his body. I couldn't relate to him anymore. When I thought about the fact that I had done this to preserve our relationship, I had to shake my head because our relationship was dying anyway.

When I arrived at her office, I was extremely apprehensive. I looked around the beige colored office. Contrary to the television portrayal of a shrink's office, there was no couch for you to lie on and talk your problems away. Also, they don't do a lot of talking; they do a lot of listening. She walked into the room about five minutes after I arrived. I looked at my watch hoping that my hour didn't start until she got there. I chose to sit in the deep, plunging beige chair because I liked the arms on it and it looked uncomfortable, and that was exactly how I felt.

"Hello, my name is Charlotte Mason but you may call me Char. I will be your counselor for the duration of your treatment. Your company pays for the first eight sessions but you may continue at your own expense beyond that, if necessary."

She seemed pleasant enough. She smiled amicably revealing the gap between her two front teeth. The gap definitely added to her alluring beauty, she had an exotic look, like she was Mediterranean.

I decided right then and there that I needed to do my best to get "fixed" within eight sessions. All I knew was that something had to give. I was dying inside and it was my fault. I couldn't get past the hurt and pain. I couldn't relieve the pressure that my actions were now causing in my life. I did all of this to keep my relationship with Trenton alive but I couldn't stand the sight of him. I didn't want him to touch me. I barely spent anytime with him. My life was a mess. I sure hoped that Char was up for what was coming her way.

As Char prepared to speak, I caught a lump in my throat. So afraid that she would judge me suddenly I didn't want to tell her what I was there for. She could sense my discomfort; she reached over to touch my hand.

"Hello, I am here to guide you. I want to put you at ease and lessen the pressure that you are feeling right now. Everything you share with me is completely confidential. No one will ever know what we discuss. Do you have any questions for me?" She was staring into my soul.

I shook my head. "No." I said, barely audibly.

"Okay, then. Let me ask you a question?"

I looked up at her. I didn't make direct eye contact because I didn't know yet if I could trust Char but I gave the appearance to be looking at her head on. "Yes. Sure, that's why I am here." I tried to lighten the mood.

"Are you a believer?"

Stupid me. The light was on but I wasn't home. "A believer of what?"

"Oh, I'm sorry. Do you believe in God?"

"Of course," I responded confidently. Who didn't believe in God?

"Is Jesus Christ your Lord and Savior? Do you believe that He died to bare your sins?"

"Yes," I said confidently again. I truly believed that. Right now, I was not living a lifestyle that He would be pleased with, but at the end of the day, I did believe in Jesus. I guess some would say that I was currently living as a backslider.

"Okay, great. I am a Christian and I would like to counsel you from that perspective, if that is okay. I can keep our sessions strictly non-religious if you prefer." She looked up at me again.

I said nothing, just thought to myself. *Okay, God. What are you doing*?

Char cleared her throat. "Do you pray?"

"I do when I am in a jam." I answered without even thinking. It was the truth.

"Okay." She said her voice very calm and steady. "Is it okay if I treat you with a Christian guidance system?"

"Yes, that is okay. I do pray sometimes. But my prayer life is not consistent. I mean, I go to church on Sunday but that is about it. I don't typically read the Bible or spend anytime with God unless I need something."

I was there to get help, so honesty was important. Besides, I didn't know this woman. It seemed easy to share my life, the good, bad and the ugly with her.

"Okay. I appreciate your honesty. Well, I would like to invite you to pick up a Bible off the coffee table and just put it in your lap. That way, as you see fit, feel free to use the table of contents to reference the scriptures that I am going to share with you."

"Okay," I smiled nervously. *Is Bible study what I need to get fixed*? I asked myself. If that was the case, I could start attending the one at church.

"Are you ready to begin?"

I nodded.

"Great, what brings you in to see me?"

Immediately, my eyes started to sting as I fought back the tears that were on their way. One got loose and traveled the lonely, bumpy road to the bottom of my left cheek. I had been breaking out lately because of all the stress in my life. I had also lost an enormous amount of weight because I couldn't keep anything on my stomach. I took a deep breath and cleared my throat.

"I had an abortion a month ago and I can't seem to get it together. I'm breaking out and I keep throwing up. I don't know how to make it stop. I had the abortion because my boyfriend made me. He wasn't ready to be a father and I feel horrible because I chose him over my baby and now I can't even stand the sight of him. I thought the abortion was the right choice because we could get pregnant later in life and we could focus on getting to know each other better and developing a strong relationship. But I can't get past what he made me do. And even though I can't stand the sight of him, I have convinced myself that I need him to survive."

I took a breath. I feared stopping to breathe midway because I might have lost my nerve to continue. It was all out there now.

She didn't even bat her eyes. She was writing vigorously on her steno pad. "Okay. Thank you for sharing. I can feel your pain as you share what is going on in your life. I am here to help you get through this tough time. I would like to impart some hope to you. This is not the end of your life or the end of the world. I don't want to belittle your experience but the best is yet to come. I assure you, you can get through this. Okay, before I go anything further, let's read what the Lord has to say. The first scripture I want to have you read is I John 1:9. Can you find that in the Bible?"

It took me a minute but I didn't even pretend like I knew where anything was, instead I was obedient and went straight for the table of contents as Char suggested. "I've got it."

"Okay, let's read it together out loud." She paused and looked up at me for confirmation.

I nodded. "If we confess our sins, He is faithful and just to forgive us of our sins and cleanse us from all unrighteousness." She looked up at me. "So, what does the passage mean to you?"

I sighed. "I guess it basically is saying that when we ask God to forgive us for the mistakes we make, He will do it and make us feel better." I smiled. Then I frowned. "But I confessed and asked God to forgive me before I even had the abortion but I do not feel better. I feel guilty. I feel like I made a terrible mistake."

"Okay, I understand how you may feel. You are right, almost. His forgiveness is not so that we feel better. His forgiveness is based on His grace and mercy. His forgiveness fulfills His Word and promise to us. He sent his son Jesus into the world to bare the sins of you and me. Jesus died so that you could have a life filled with abundance. God's grace and mercy is what enables us to move on and move forward. The way you feel about what happened is a personal issue. You have to forgive yourself. Arguably, it will be much harder for you to forgive yourself than it was for God. He has already forgiven you for having the abortion. When Jesus died on the cross for your sins and mine, he took the sting out of death and made it so that we could still exist even when we behave in a manner not pleasing to God. But the Bible never says that we will feel better as soon as we confess our sins." Char chuckled lightly.

"I understand. So how do I get free?" I asked.

"Where the spirit of the Lord is, there is liberty. If the spirit of the Lord is not with you, you will not feel free from the burden. If you want to feel better, get to know the Lord, for real. Get to know the Holy Spirit. God is a jealous lover. He does not like to share and if you only commit to spending time with Him on Sunday, he is not happy about that. He wants to be your everything." She paused and looked at me before she continued. "It will be important that you take a look at Philippians 3:13, 14." She paused and looked at me.

"Do you want me to check that one now?" I asked, preparing to turn to Philippians in the Bible.

"We will look at that passage in a second. First, let's go back to the first scripture explanation. I wanted you to read that scripture because the first thing you need to do is pray to the Lord with a sincere heart so that He knows that you are sorry for having an abortion. While you are confessing that, why not also confess the premarital relations and lies that put you in that condition." She looked up at me. I think she could sense my embarrassment. "Now, I don't say that in judgment of you, but I am going to be honest and suggest that first confessing the sin will begin your process of healing. God is merciful. If He wanted you dead because you had an abortion, trust me, you would be. And since that is not the case, feel confident in the fact that you have an opportunity to start all over by simply confessing your sin and getting cleansed by the Lord. You have got to forgive yourself and release the burden on your heart. Once you do that, you will be able to move on. And you will be able to move on with your boyfriend, if that is your desire. An abortion is not the end of the world. I know it seems tough right now, but there is a light at the end of the tunnel."

I could not see the light. I prayed that the light would come on.

"Now, let's take a look at Philippians."

I turned to the scripture and started reading it aloud. "Brothers, I do not consider myself yet to have taken hold of it. But this one thing I do, forgetting what is behind and straining toward that which is ahead, I press on toward the goal to win the prize for which God has called me Heavenward in Christ Jesus." I finished and looked up at Char.

"What do you think?"

"I think it sounds easier than it is. I know the past is the past but the past is haunting me. How in the world am I supposed to reach toward what is ahead of me when I want to go back to the day before I had the abortion? And I wanted to go back even further to all of the other mistakes that I have made and even the wrongs that have been done to me." I was crying again.

"Prayer is the key. Write down Philippians 4: 6. I want you to read that at home tonight. I encourage you to start keeping a journal. Each day, right down how you feel. Keep the journal with you at all times. If you are in your car at a traffic light and you have an emotional breakdown, journal how you felt and what you think triggered the episode. Since we will only meet weekly it will be important that you use your journal as a mechanism of self-healing by getting your feelings out of your head. I read in your profile that you have no one to share your grief with except your boyfriend Trenton and the two of you aren't getting along right now, correct?"

"Yes, that is correct. I am completely alone in this. Trenton does not understand what I am going through. His lack of understanding leads to arguments. I have nowhere else to turn." I sniffled a little and wiped my eyes.

"You do have one other place to turn, turn to the Lord. You can talk to God just like you are speaking with me right now. Tell Him how you feel, share your feelings, hurts, disappointments, and successes, you can and should share everything with Him. Also, the journal will be a great outlet for you. It may even give you something to talk to Trenton about when the dust has settled. That's it for today; I'll see you next week. Keep the journal of your thoughts and we will discuss anything you need to next week."

That was a quick session. I had no idea how I was going to get "fixed" in just eight of them when they went so fast.

I went home and read that scripture: *Do not be anxious about anything, but in everything, by prayer and petition, with thanksgiving, present your requests to God. Philippians 4:6.*

Initially I wasn't sure how going to therapy was going to work; but, I went back anyway to the other seven sessions and by the end I had forgiven myself and gotten one step closer to the Lord in the process. Once I was able to live again, I was able to breathe on my own without the fear that the bottom would fall out of my life. I also had quite a few journals.

My skin cleared up and my self-confidence increased. It was a slow process and those first eight weeks helped a lot. I could feel the pressure releasing on my heart. I allowed myself to consider the possibility that I could be renewed and freed from my past. I was able to eat food without rushing into the bathroom.

I continued seeing Char even after the company paid time expired. I really grew to like her. She is still my therapist to this day. Because of her influence, I was definitely intrigued about a living a life for God. Sadly, I admit to you that I didn't immediately alter my lifestyle just because He forgave me. I continued to allow myself to be bound by my own issues. I realized that recovery started with me and as long as I held myself responsible for the past, it would hinder my future.

Chapter 15

If we confess our sins, he is faithful and just to forgive us our sins and cleanse us from all unrighteousness.

I John 1:9

Once I lifted the burden of my personal paralysis, I could see the haze over my life start to clear. With the shackles off my mind, I was no longer sitting in the prison of my soul for aborting my first child. Trenton and I stopped fighting about the abortion and started focusing on the future.

Things with Trenton got back on track but I had decided that we were not going to have a physically intimate relationship going forward. I did not like to think about his hands touching me. Once I threw up just thinking about having relations with him. My head was so screwed up. Even after the therapy, I still couldn't deal with some things, things that concerned Trenton and our relationship.

Yet, I couldn't muster up the courage to walk away. Honestly, I had no reason to stay but the pull he had on me at that time was like a moth to a flame. I felt like he owed me something. He held my expectation of reciprocity in the palm of his hands because I had given him the power to control my heart. But him touching me, that repulsed me. I decided that we would focus on getting to know each other and being friends instead of further complicating our coexistence. It was the best way to keep me out of the hell I had just experienced. He claimed to have understood and I promised to be appropriately affectionate. But even at the thought of kissing him and holding his hands, I was uneasy.

We began to increase the amount of time we spent together and it was again getting easier to share in small moments of happiness with him. I really did love his smile. It illuminated the room; it illuminated my heart like the bright sun on a new day. It was vivid, warm and welcoming, like the smell of a load of clothes right out of the dryer with a hint of lavender fabric softener.

The Sunday following my last company paid counseling session, I went to my church without a chip on my shoulder. I felt a sense of pride in praising and worshipping the Lord. I finally felt like I deserved the opportunity to get into His presence. For so long, I had been on the outside looking in because of my own self-pity and guilt. But that day, I was truly glad that I could rejoice in the day that the Lord had made. I had been released to get back to life, as I knew it.

I was also excited because we were having a world-renowned guest preacher. He was a Bishop known for his ability to offer prophesy to the people of God. I couldn't wait to hear him preach, as I had watched him on TV every Thursday night for the past year. He had fast become one of my favorites. He was young and his sermons were always geared toward my generation giving us a message that we could understand and subscribe to.

The one thing I had always disliked about the church I grew up in was that the Word went so far over my head there was no way it could penetrate my heart. I always got so frustrated because the message was not on my level.

I had to get to the church a little early to be able to get a seat in the main sanctuary. World-renowned preachers always drew a big crowd and I wanted to be part of the action. Sitting in the overflow room was like sitting in the hallway. The screens were delayed. I needed to be upfront and center.

I climbed the steps to the sanctuary and found a seat quickly not far from where I usually sat. I people watched as they filtered in. I could feel the buzz of excitement at the Bishop's impending visit. Brother Booker got on the keyboard and started playing the first song and the choir came marching in, spilling up both side aisles simultaneously.

Everyone stood for the entrance of the choir; they were singing *Total Praise* by Richard Smallwood. They sang the first verse and the reprise three times as they took their places in the choir stand. I just loved the end with the "Amen's" in each part and then together in harmony. It was beautiful and I got teary-eyed at the words. After the last set of "Amen's," they started in on the first verse again.

I sang the words in my heart as the choir sang. They sang the reprise a few more times before they began with the Fred Hammond spirit filled song *Let the Praise Begin.*

About a half an hour later, the Pastor, the Bishop and his entourage made their entrance. I had never seen so many people. I think I counted twenty people who walked in behind the Bishop. He, of course, sat in the pulpit while his groupies filled up the front two pews. Next thing you know, praise and worship took on another level and the choir soloist took the microphone and began singing her heart out. I had to stand up on the song she sang. Wow, I got teary-eyed as I thought about the power of God.

There is no greater love than a man who would lay down his life for his friends.

She hit all the right notes and soothed my soul with her melodious voice. Each note touched my spirit and gave me goose bumps. He had sure enough forgiven me for my sins and He was working things out in my life. He had laid down His life for me. I thanked Him silently.

A few more songs were sung to round out praise and worship and then it was time for the preached Word.

The Bishop took his place at the podium and began to belt out his message. "Somebody ought to praise the Lord in this place. I said somebody ought to praise the Lord." The sanctuary went wild. Then all of a sudden, he was out of the pulpit and down on the floor laying hands on people and ushering in the praise of the Lord. People were getting healed right in front of me. The "shouting music" was being played on the keyboards as he said pivotal words. I watched in awe of what was going on; simultaneously hoping that he would come nowhere near me. I had always been afraid of the power of the Lord. I think it was because I just didn't understand and ignorance was bliss, but nonetheless, it scared the living daylights out of me.

As if he heard the conversation going on in my head, he called me out.

He looked right at me and into the microphone he shouted, "God wants your full attention, girl. You, right there in the pink dress." I pointed at myself.

He said, "Yeah, you. Come here. I have a word for you from the Lord."

I was so nervous; I didn't want to go up there. Like he could sense my hesitation, he climbed on the pew and walked pew by pew over to me until he stood right in front of me, standing on the pew just ahead of mine.

He pointed at me and said, "The spirit of the Lord is on you girl. There is such an anointing on your life. Even though you just did something that makes you ashamed,

God loves you and He is covering your spirit even now. He forgives you, now you must forgive yourself and walk into what He has for you. God sent me to tell you to guard yourself. It is very important that you watch who you allow into your space. Don't try to befriend everybody. Even those who are your friends now, check them out. If they don't line up, get rid of them. If you don't take inventory of your associations, you will lose a great deal. People will try to steal your birthright and what God has planned for you. Everyone won't be able to understand who you are and what God has purposed in your spirit. There will be much opposition as you align yourself with God's will. Although you love attention and need people around you to be secure, be careful. If you are not careful, you will lose your standing. Everybody isn't supposed to be your friend. Guard your associations so that you can walk into what God has for you. Heed my word, saith the Lord. Receive and be blessed."

With that, he reached out his hand and barely touched me and I fell to the floor. He didn't push me or forced me down like I had always thought they did, he simply laid his hand on my head, and very lightly I might add, but I instantly felt the power of his anointing and it sent me down to eat a carpet sandwich. It took me a few minutes to get myself together.

I couldn't believe what he told me. *I needed to check my associations, was He talking about Trenton*? All of a sudden, I felt a huge release in my spirit. Tears flowed from my heart. The tears flowing from my heart were grateful for God's favor over my life.

"Thank you Lord," I shouted at the top of my lungs.

I was so glad that despite what I had just done, the Lord still had something to say to me. I was so elated about the surge of the spirit that I felt radiating through me. My tears were replaced with a smile that resonated a bright brilliance, a bright beam of light. I was beside myself so much so that it was hard for me to focus on the message that the Bishop preached. I had heard a Word from the Lord.

After church was over, I said my hellos and other pleasantries and kept it moving. It was amazing to me how I was no longer carrying the burden that had followed me through the door. I felt free. It was then that I knew for sure that God had forgiven me for ending the life He had given me.

I knew that if God could forgive me, I could forgive Trenton. And so I did. I started the process of allowing our relationship to heal. I knew that he had made a mistake; but so had I. Who was I to act as if his mistake was greater than that of my own?

As I reflect back on all that had happened, I now realize that God had again put the writing on the wall to tell me to move swiftly and leave Trenton behind. Trenton was one of those associations that didn't line up. Because I was not in my rightful place, I did not heed the clear warning God had delivered for me. Remember, we hear what we want to hear when the Lord is speaking to us. Can I get an Amen?

Chapter 16

For his anger lasts only a moment, but his favor lasts a lifetime; weeping may remain for a night, but rejoicing comes in the morning.

Psalm 30:5

"Trenton," I called from the kitchen. "Can you come in here a second?"

I was making a new dish for dinner and I needed him to taste the sauce.

"Hey, babe."

He leaned in to kiss me on the cheek. For the first time in a while, I didn't wince at the thought of his lips on my body. I smiled at him. It felt good to smile and mean it.

"Taste this." I demanded. "I need to know if it has the right mixture of sweet and spicy."

I playfully shoved the spoon into his mouth.

"Oh, yeah. This is good. I can't wait for dinner."

I smiled and thought about from whence we came. It had been a long time since we had been able to exist in the same space without tension about what we had already been through. I was truly glad that we had been able to move past our blemish.

My thoughts were interrupted when the phone rang. We were at his house, so I didn't even move in the direction of the phone.

"Hello," he answered on the third ring. "Oh, hey. What's going on? Really? Oh yeah, that's what's up. Yeah, I am definitely trying to get there. Let me check and I'll call you back to let you know for sure."

He walked back into the kitchen and gave me a hug from behind. I smiled lightly. Somehow I knew that the hug I had just received was a build up for something. I was right.

"Who was that on the phone?" I asked. I did my best not to sound too meddlesome.

"It was Constance." He turned away.

"Who's Constance?" I repositioned myself to stand in front of him.

"She is a fellow trustee from church. She got an extra ticket to see Grover Washington, Jr. for Friday night. She wanted to see if I was interested in it."

"How did she react when you said no?"

"I didn't give her an answer. I told her I would let her know." He was looking at me as if I had three heads.

"Why did you do that?"

"Because I wanted to talk with you about it before I gave her an answer."

"So who else is going? Either that, or she has two tickets, one for you and *me*." There was no way that I was going to agree to him going on a date with someone else. I rolled my eyes; this time, I turned away.

It was his turn to reposition himself so that he faced me. "What's that about?" He glared at me.

"Well, I don't know this Constance and she is calling you, a man in an exclusive relationship, to invite you to use her extra ticket. That's not cool. Why does she think it is okay to call you?"

I was not feeling this whole exchange. I didn't feel good about it.

"It's not like that, we are just friends. We count money together on Sundays after church and to pass the time, we chat about stuff. I happened to mention that I love jazz and she expressed a love for it as well. I never thought anything would come of it, but you know how much I love him."

"When did you have this conversation? Who else counts money? Who was a trustee first?" I was building a case with my constant questions.

"We had this conversation last Sunday after the second service. It was just she and I; we only count two at a time. We have a rotating schedule. I was a trustee first. She became one a month or so after me."

It was Wednesday. And it seemed to me that maybe she only became a trustee to get closer to Trenton.

"And magically, three days later, she has an extra ticket. Did you even know he was in town? I don't know Trenton, this sounds fishy to me."

I didn't like how my stomach knotted as we were talking. My spirit was fired up and not in a good way. I was really trying not to "trip" but I didn't like this one bit.

"Come on, you are making a big deal about nothing. It's innocent," he pleaded.

"So that's it." I was pissed. Just when things were looking up…we were getting back on track. Here he was defending this Constance and her desire to take him on a date.

"You know, you are a grown man and I cannot tell you what to do, but I don't like it. I think that it is disrespectful that she would even do that knowing you have a girlfriend. And if she calls herself your friend, she needs to respect the boundaries that go with friendship."

Then I thought, maybe she doesn't know. "She does know, doesn't she?"

"Of course she does. I tell everyone about my baby." He said as he scooped me in for a big kiss.

He was trying to divert my attention from the matter at hand but I wasn't having that. I dodged his kiss and glared at him.

"Seriously, who else is going?" I asked.

"Her mother and aunt are also going." He said kind of matter-of-fact like.

Great, I thought. "So, she's inviting you to meet her family. Trenton, I don't know about this. No, scratch that. I do know about this. I do not like it," I said very assertively as I enunciated each word.

"Don't you trust me?" He pulled my face real close to his. I could smell the remnants of the sweet & spicy sauce on his breath.

"Let me ask you this, Bob calls and asks me to go with him to see Anita Baker, who I love beyond words. He only had one ticket and you've never met Bob. Are you going to be okay with me going?"

"Yes, because I trust you."

"You are a liar. You know good and well you are not going to let some man take me anywhere."

"If you really wanted to go, because I trust you I would. Don't you trust me?"

"It's not about whether or not I trust you, it's that I don't know her and I do not feel comfortable with my man being out with another woman and her family that I do not know. I don't trust her. She seems shady to me. Why wouldn't she find a girlfriend to take the extra ticket? Why ask you?"

"I don't know why she did. But I do know that she doesn't have a lot of friends and that is why she has reached out to me. She is just a friend. Trust me; it is nothing more than that. I don't care about her family being at the concert, I am just excited about seeing Grover."

"I can't tell you what to do, but I can tell you that I am not comfortable with it. If you chose to go, that's on you; but know that I don't like it."

With that, I turned back to the meal I was preparing. I opened the oven door and could hear the chicken sizzling; it was ready for the sauce to be poured on top to make the glaze.

We ate dinner that night in a sea of unresolved silence. The waves of unsettled concerns were billowing back and forth without a break; my seat felt uncomfortable. If you listened, you could hear my pain in each wave. I was hurting at the thought that he saw no reason for alarm. You could hear the unresolved stress and angst. It was so tense that even my great cooking couldn't lighten the mood.

After we ate dinner, I left Trenton to clean up and went home. As I drove home, my blood was boiling. Here I was trying to get past the last blemish on the face of our relationship and before it cleared up completely, a new one was coming in. But this blemish had a name and it was Constance. I couldn't believe that he was seriously considering going on a date with her.

Was I right to call it a date? Well, if it looks like a duck and quacks like a duck, it must be a duck. Constance was an ugly duckling.

As I walked in the door, my home phone was ringing. I got to it just before the call went to voicemail.

"Hello," I said in a hurried tone of voice.

"Hey babe, it's me. I wanted to make sure you made it home. Also, I wanted to let you know that I heard what you said today, but I think it is harmless. I cannot miss an opportunity to be 3rd row center in front of my favorite jazz musician. I promise I will go to the concert and then I will come straight home," he pleaded again.

"You heard what I said and have chosen to disregard it?"

"It's not like that, babe."

"Whatever."

"What does that mean?" He said, in a flippant tone of voice. I could tell he was agitated.

"How are you getting there?"

"We are going to ride together."

"Oh, so it *is* a date. Need I remind you that you have a girlfriend?" I said, my voice rising. I continued without giving him a chance to respond. "So you think that right after the concert they will bring you home instead of grabbing something to eat? After driving all the way to Philly to the *Comcast Center*? Right. I am sure everyone else in the car will be okay with getting you right back to your girlfriend, who was stupid enough to agree to allow you to go on a date with another woman, in Delaware. You know what, Trenton. Do whatever you want. I don't have time to argue with you when you are going to do what you want despite how I feel about the matter. Okay. Listen, I've got to go. I just walked in the door and there are *important* things I need to handle." With that, I hung up the phone.

I was determined not to give any more credence to that conversation or the entire situation. Clearly, he didn't care about my feelings after all we'd been through. There was nothing I could do to change the mind of a man whose mind was made up.

As I looked back, again I found myself asking *why was I still with him*? I mean, my stay was long over due. The writing was on the wall. Apparently in invisible ink. How I missed the signs was beyond me. I guess the love dust really had my view distorted.

I wanted to give Constance a piece of my mind but she was only doing what she felt it was okay to do. Clearly Trenton led her to believe that such behavior was okay.

I was going to Trenton's church on Sunday so that I could make my presence known. *I hope it's not too late*, I thought to myself. That was the first I heard of her, but it certainly wasn't the last.

Very soon there after, I heard her name more times than I ever cared to. I remember one night when we were asleep that he got a late night phone call and jumped up to go to her rescue. She had allegedly gotten a flat tire and she couldn't find anyone else to call. He went to her aid and I was the fool because I just thought that he was being a brother in Christ.

The day following the late night tire change, my mother and I were riding to *Happy Harry's* and I was so upset. My mother tried to comfort me but I couldn't shake the feeling in the pit of my stomach and even when I heard my mother say those words that I am sure I believed were true, I defended his honor.

"You are not going to like what I have to tell you." My mother said.

I cut my eyes in her direction. "What?"

"He's messing with that old woman."

"Mom, how can you call her old?"

"Because she is too old for him, that's why. She's almost my age. And that is just nasty. She truly ought to be ashamed of herself. Maybe I should have a few choice words with her."

My mother was 48 at the time.

"No, Mom he's not. They are friends and he is just being a good friend. There is no reason for me to be worried. Besides, I trust him. He loves me. He has given my no reason to not trust him fully. Don't worry."

"What does love have to do with anything when a man is being pursued by a persistent woman and she is creating reasons for them to be together?"

I didn't respond, instead I looked out the passenger side car window. We drove the rest of the ride in silence but I knew even then that she was right, but I couldn't face the music.

Couldn't? Didn't want to was more like it.

Chapter 17

O my God, I cry out by day, but you do not answer, by night and am not silent.

Psalm 22:2

It was Saturday morning before I knew it. I know they say "time flies when you're having fun;" but it keeps moving even when you're not. I was still very down. My heart hurt so bad that I thought I would just keel over and die. That would certainly feel better than living with the pain.

As I thought that, instantly, God's Word reminded me that His spirit was renewing me. The thought of that lifted me a little. It was true that I knew that God was at work. Despite the fact that I didn't do much for Him, He was still showing me His favor. The fact that this all happened before the altar was far better than me ending up in jail after the wedding.

If Constance had shown up to my wedding (to which she wasn't invited) pregnant with Trenton's child, I would have certainly been on my way to "three hots and a cot." I chuckled.

I could see the newscast now, "Bride caught in a disastrous fight with a pregnant woman, it didn't end well.

Full story at eleven." I smiled broadly. I would have worn her out.

If I could have found any reason to go over there and take my anger out on her I would. Not that I wanted Trenton, but for sheer principle. But I knew that she would press charges, and I wasn't going to jail for anybody.

"Oh well," I shrugged and decided to get on with my day.

I had a lot to do around the house and I was meeting Tracey for breakfast. Two and a half days of crying and rehashing the past hadn't gotten me anywhere but upset. I was still mad as hell.

I checked the clock, it was six-thirty. I looked at the clock on my nightstand again to make sure I read it correctly and sighed. Realizing that there was no time to turn over for another snooze period on the alarm clock, I decided to jump up and face the day. It would be my first day out of the house since the break up.

I wandered into the bathroom and looked at my face in the mirror, one word: yuck. I had tearstains all over the place and there were several spots where my hair was stuck together by what appeared to be dried up snot. The eyeliner and mascara that I had been wearing on Wednesday had produced black railroad tracks around my eyes and vertically along the path marked by what I would have guessed to be the first tearstains.

Yes, just as you are thinking, I hadn't washed a muscle in two and a half days. I had been stewing in my own pity and somehow smelling like day old uncooked meat made the feeling more authentic. What love made me do?

I turned on the shower, took off my Wednesday work clothes, pantyhose and all, and prepared to get it. Just before I stepped inside the scolding hot shower, I decided that I would lighten my mood with a little music, which had always been my therapy. A good song would make my spirit feel light and calm.

I tiptoed into the hallway and into my bedroom to turn on my CD player. There were three CDs in the changer and I really didn't remember what I had been listening to last.

Surprise me, I thought as I ran back in to hit the shower.

Just as I stepped inside, the music enveloped me. I heard Kirk Franklin and the Family singing *My Life is in Your Hands*. Truthfully, my life was in His hands. It had to be. There was no way that I could face the world without the Lord with me.

I let the water from my massaging shower head fall on me. As it fell, I once again, started to cry.

I trust you, Lord; I cried.

This time my tears took me back to the night when I was so excited to share the great news of my promotion to Assistant Vice President with Trenton but I couldn't find him anywhere. He wasn't answering his home or cell phone. I had always been a worrywart so when I couldn't get him on the phone after multiple attempts, I got in my car and drove to his place. I parked around the corner so he wouldn't be alerted to my presence before he walked in the door. I sat in the dark for several hours.

Even as I sat there waiting for him to come home, I wondered *why am I going through all this trouble*? This was too much. But it didn't propel me to leave. Are you asking yourself why?

Even though I had talked myself into leaving many times, I never got up the nerve to leave. I somehow felt that since he made me abort our child he owed me. He owed me the life I had always wanted. So, stuck on stupid, I sat and waited for him to come home. And stuck on stupid, I waited for him to give me what he owed me. When he finally did show up, it was well after 2 am. I was asleep on the couch by then.

To this day, I have never gotten what he owed me.

"Oh, hey baby. What are you doing here?" Trenton said. He looked startled that I was in his living room. "I didn't see your car." He added.

"I parked around the corner," I paused. "There weren't any spots out front when I got here." I lied. Trenton had me doing a lot of that. The thought that I even cared enough to lie made me upset. But I played my role.

"Where've you been?" I asked.

"I was out with a friend." He answered flippantly.

When a man says "a friend" he is referring to the opposite sex. If he were out with his boys, he'd simply say, "my boys" or the name of the guy friend.

"A friend that pees standing up or sitting down?" I countered. But, of course, I knew the answer. He was with Constance.

"Both. I met up with my friends from MD. But as the evening wore on, just Mike and I remained. I didn't know you were coming over. I would have come by your place. We were at *Timothy's* in Newark. Why didn't you call me?"

"Where's your phone?" Again, I knew the answer. He hadn't a bit more looked at his phone than the man in the moon.

"Right here, why?" He said looking down at it. "Oh, you did call me and *seven* times." Trenton sounded agitated.

I could sense a little attitude as he remarked at how many times I'd called. I refrained from giving him a piece of my mind at that very second but I was close to breaking.

"First of all, I can call you as often as I like. Second of all, I wanted to talk with you and since it is not like you to not answer your phone, I got worried." I found myself defending why I had stalked him that evening. I didn't believe that he was out with Mike though.

"Did something happen? Is everything all right?" He asked, trying to sound concerned. I didn't buy it.

"Why are you concerned now, it is 2 am and you didn't even as much as call me today. If something had happened, I wouldn't have been able to find you and it wouldn't matter now."

Something told me that he was not with Mike and it was bothering me. "So, you weren't with Constance?" I braced myself for the worse.

"She ended up stopping by the bar a little later, why?" He said very nonchalantly.

I could tell he was really focusing to take the emotion out of his voice.

"How did she know that you were there?"

"She called me while I was out."

So he had taken her call but not mine. "Oh, so I guess she is on the VIP. Do you want to be with her? I can let you go if you'd like me to."

I didn't mean that. *You are a sucker*. I scolded myself.

"Why would you say that? She sat there with Mike and me and had a couple of drinks. It isn't that serious."

The phone rang.

"Hello," he answered. His body stiffened when he realized who was on the other end of the phone. It must have been *her*.

"Okay, good. Let me talk to you later. Good Night." He hurriedly hung up the phone.

He avoided my eyes as he hung up the phone. Why did she think it was okay to call my man's house at 2 am? I needed to know that. If I hadn't of been there, would they have talked longer?

I was two seconds from her behind. I needed help; this man had me wanting to fight.

"So who was that at this time of night?" I knew the answer. Constance was constantly getting on my nerves.

He coughed, "I'm sorry what did you say?"

I rolled my eyes. "You heard me, who is calling your house at 2 am?" This time, I was indignant.

Why had he tried to evade my question?

"It was Constance letting me know she made it home safely," he said in a monotone voice.

"Why is she telling you?" I had a serious attitude. I crossed my arms and peered at him. My eyes were burning into his flesh.

"I didn't like the idea of her driving herself home; she had a few drinks more than her limit."

He knew her limit? I asked myself. "And how do you know her limit?" I asked.

He seemed so concerned about her. "We have been through this before, she and I are friends. I can't change that. We are trustees together. We travel in the same circles from time to time. We like the same things. I am not going to keep apologizing for it or keep having this conversation with you," he screamed.

I felt myself backing down when he raised his voice. He had been drinking and there was that one time….

"Okay, fine, Trenton. Promise me one thing…"

"What do you want, now?" He continued to rant. I could tell that he had also had a drink or two beyond his limit.

"Tell me that you haven't slept with her. I'm no fool. I know that she is constantly throwing herself at you, pun intended. Promise me that you have been true to me." I searched his slanted eyes for assurance; I came up empty.

"How dare you ask me that? You know good and well the answer to that question. But if I have to say it, no, I have never slept with her."

"He avoided looking at me head on before he took that deep breath. Once he did, he searched my eyes for understanding. And added, "I wouldn't do that to you." With that, he grabbed my head and kissed me roughly.

I am not sure if I was satisfied with his answer but I let it slide. As I looked at him in his eyes, it appeared that he was telling me the truth. I pulled out of his rough embrace, whispered some excuse and let myself out. There was no way I was going to stay with him on a night that he had been drinking. I was not going to be his fool again.

Chapter 18

For the Lord hath called thee as a woman forsaken and grieved in spirit...

Isaiah 54:6a

With the music still blaring in the background, I emerged from the shower. The steam had fogged the bathroom mirror, so I took my right hand and wiped away the thin layer of film on the mirror to reveal my swollen face. I had hoped that a shower would make me feel better, look better and lighten my load, but it didn't. It was still there; lingering and creating emptiness that had me questioning my every move.

Something was missing and for the first time since Wednesday, I truly knew it wasn't Trenton. Love didn't live here anymore and I was okay that it had moved with no forwarding address. I knew clearly and as sure as I was born that I didn't want his lying, cheating behind anywhere near me.

Instantly, I felt a release. It hit me like a ton of bricks. Just thinking over all that had happened; I realized that I was so glad that I had that abortion. If I hadn't, I would be caught like a rock in a hard place right now trying to explain to a child why mommy and daddy were not going to be together anymore.

Thank you Lord for sparing me from that horror, I said inwardly, hoping that God heard me.

I was still so ashamed about the fact that I had allowed our relationship to go on for so many years.

I had become like a lot of women I knew; I let him swallow my existence. I completely submerged myself in him to the point that I didn't know where I ended and he began. I had been so blind to think that we could have our happy ending. I had been so stupid to think that he was any different. Like lots of women I knew, I overlooked the evidence that he didn't love me, really love me like it mattered. I allowed myself to be inconvenienced for the sake of staying in a relationship. I told myself that having a bad man was better than not having one at all.

I believed all those lies for so long. It all stemmed from me not loving myself enough. Self-love is so important, this self-reflection helped me to realize.

Self-love is what makes us press toward the mark of the high calling in Christ, I thought to myself.

As I drove the twenty minutes to the restaurant, silence surrounded me. I really needed to steady myself. I kept reliving Wednesday night in my head. I really didn't want to get into it at the restaurant. The Post House wasn't your typical restaurant. There were no booths to separate you from the other patrons. They had a long counter with stools and Tracey and I would just select two, order our delicious pancakes and keep it moving. We'd be on display for everyone coming in to see. I had promised her that after we ate, I would drive the short distance back to her place to talk with her. I knew that Tracey would ease my pain.

I pulled in the parking lot a few minutes after we agreed to meet.

I opened the door and briefly surveyed the counter, I saw Tracey sitting to the left with my stool reserved beside her, her chocolate brown leather purse sitting on top of the tattered navy blue leather fabric covering the swiveling stool.

"Hey," I said as I walked over to join her.

"Hey. How are you?" She smiled at me.

"Girl." It was all I could get out before a persistent tear made its escape. I was determined to have that be the only one, for now at least. I looked at her with as much sanity as I could muster.

I was going crazy inside. I was everywhere at once. I could only live one minute at a time. I had been so full and strong when I left my house but somewhere between the house and the car, the script flipped and I was a basket case again. Unfortunately, it didn't flip back when I got out of the car and entered the restaurant so I was one comment away from crying a river. Thank God for skin otherwise I'd be a puddle on the floor.

"I am making it. I am already all right." *Speak life to your life*, I told myself.

"Oh, is there anything I can do?" Tracey smiled and touched my shoulder to let me know that she meant it.

"Girl, just keep praying for me. I need all the strength I can get to come my way." I said with all the sincerity I could muster.

"I know that's right. Plus, you'll get some good Word tomorrow. My Pastor is no joke. He makes it plain and tells it right." She smiled at me.

I winced inwardly. *Was I ready for some real Word*?

"Did you order yet?" I decided to change the subject to prevent a flood from coming.

"No, I was waiting for you. But I guess I could've. We always get the same thing," she giggled.

I was so glad to be having normal conversation again. I must admit, it felt good.

I kept glancing around to make sure that I didn't see anyone I knew while we were in the restaurant. We were so close to Trenton's church and a lot of the members lived in a close proximity and any of them could love the Post House as much as I.

I knew by now they all knew what had happened. I think they knew before I did and those "saints" didn't care to bring me into the loop. I didn't feel up to answering any questions or pretending like life was still great. I really wanted to fly under the radar. That's why, I, a woman who didn't usually choose a baseball cap as a part of her wardrobe, was donning one that day. Incognito was the way to go. It hid my eyes. They were still very swollen from the personal floods that had become a staple in my life.

Tracey looked my way and gave me a reassuring smile. I think she noticed my nervous demeanor. "You know, I think that it is important that you spend some time reading the Word. In Philippians chapter four Paul tells us: Be anxious of nothing, but in all things through prayer and supplication make your requests known to God." It was all she said but she knew that it was just enough to calm my spirit and allow me to enjoy our time together.

I smiled back to reassure her that I got her point. I just needed to have a little talk with Jesus. The only problem was that I had no idea where to start and what to say. Yet, somehow I knew that I would soon figure it out. I took another quick glance around the restaurant before I began to devour my fluffy pancakes. We finished our breakfast, paid the tab and headed to the parking lot.

I followed Tracey to her house so we could talk. I was bracing myself to tell the truth, the whole truth and nothing but the truth. Most people didn't know what really happened inside of our relationship. Remember, I was a faker, they learned what I wanted them to know to glorify the relationship and how happy we were. It was time to finally tell the truth.

When I left Tracey's, I was feeling much better. Talking to her was very therapeutic. I headed for the *Mercedes Benz* dealership on Lancaster Avenue. It was time for me to cash in my wedding money and I was leaving Sandy behind and I was getting an upgrade. I had my eyes on a C320 Coupe sedan and I was ready to make it happen.

As I walked into the dealership, immediately I felt the air of distinction and sophistication. There was something about the possibility of success that made a *Mercedes* appealing. And you know me, the queen of "fake it until you make it;" I had to do my part for the cause. Like I said before, I may have been miserable on the inside but I would be styling and profiling on the outside.

About an hour later, with the help of a knowledgeable sales representative, I left with a fully loaded 2002 C320 sedan that was a gold metallic color, which I named "Therapy" because between her and Char, I was going to get back on the good foot.

My next stop was taking me to see my hairdresser at the JC Penney Styling Salon in the Christiana Mall. She was going to be so surprised when I told her to cut my hair! I wanted something short, cute and flirty. The new me was long over due; she'd been stewing in her own pity since Wednesday but it was time to make an important change. I decided to wash Trenton right out of my hair.

I got excited; with Trenton gone, I had lost 185 pounds and I was getting lighter every minute.

Chapter 19

Here I am! I stand at the door and knock. If anyone hears my voice and opens the door, I will come in and eat with him, and he with me.

Revelations 3:20

When I woke up Sunday morning, I was a little nervous about going to church with Tracey. She reassured me when we talked the day before that I would feel comfortable and fit right in but I was still nervous. I stayed in the bed a little longer than my normal forty-five minutes of snooze time and tried to think of some good excuses as to why I couldn't make it to church. I don't know why I was so nervous.

I grew up in the church. I had joined two churches since I graduated from college. Granted the last church I was affiliated with was full of hypocrites who said one thing but did something entirely different, but there was no reason for me to be afraid.

I had seen people get the "Holy Ghost" and shout and praise the Lord in all kinds of funny and unusual ways. I had heard people speak in unknown tongues. Some who were truly speaking in their prayer language and some who were "comininahyundai." I had been prophesied to and watched people receive a true blessing from the Lord.

Her church was non-denominational and focused just like its name said on praise, worship and the Word of God. Basically, as she explained it to me, when the Spirit fell, anything could and probably would happen. It sounded so pure, like music to my ears. It sounded like just what I needed after all the drama and hypocrisy of the two Baptist churches of my past.

So why was I so hesitant?

I knew that her church was a place where I couldn't fade into the background. I would be a key part of everything that went on there because it was smaller than I was use to. I had always gravitated to large churches because I could blend in when I wanted to and there was no one to convict me when I was out of line and "leaning unto my own understanding."

I was still so ashamed about everything that I had done in my past up to and including my now past relationship with Trenton and I had convinced myself that if they could clearly hear from God, they would definitely know what I was going through and they would be able to call me on my mess.

And that scared me beyond belief. I didn't want people closer than I was willing for them to be and the fact that there was liberty at her church had me going crazy with fear, excitement, anticipation and angst. I was wound up in knots at the thought of not fitting in there. I was also afraid that I would love it. If I did, then I would have to live like I knew the Word of God, right? I wasn't sure if I was ready for that.

I grabbed my bathrobe and went downstairs to the kitchen to make myself a cup of tea. I knew a cup of *Lemon Zest* tea would calm my nerves. I grabbed my favorite mug, one that Trenton had given me, out of the oak colored cabinet and turned on the stove and put my wedge wood blue teapot on the burner.

I looked at the mug and got pissed all over again. I threw it against the wall and grabbed another one to hold my tea. I got my sugar canister down from the cupboard, grabbed the lemon juice from the refrigerator and waited to hear the teapot sing.

After I stirred my brew, I stepped over the shattered mug on the kitchen floor and headed for the kitchen table and pulled out a chair, reaching for the stereo remote as I also decided to turn on some gospel music to get myself in the mood. I bobbed my head at the sound of Fred Hammond's *We are Blessed* coming from my stereo system. Fred Hammond always moved me. Like he was singing, I was blessed.

As I sang along with Fred and his Radicals for Christ, I felt myself getting lighter. That gave me just what I needed to go back upstairs and get myself ready to go have a little talk with Jesus.

Chapter 20

For where two or three come together in my name, there am I with them.

Matthew 18: 20

After donning a modest light blue Capri pantsuit and matching shoes, my Bible and I piled into my brand spankin' new car, Therapy. It felt so good to be enveloped by those roomy leather seats.

Ah, I loved the new car smell.

I was feeling good about going to church now as I let the radio soothe me all the way to the church doors. Every Sunday on WDAS FM you could hear Sunday Inspirations and right then Donnie McClurkin was singing *Stand*. He was singing that after you've done all you can, you should stand. Well, I definitely received that because I had done all I could. I had tried it my way. I had failed miserably. I had done everything I felt I was big and bad enough to do and I had absolutely nothing to show for it. Well, that wasn't true; I had pain, poor self-esteem, no self-confidence, misery, betrayal, lies, a broken hurt and a wounded spirit to show for all I had done on my own. Not to mention that I was out of all my wedding non-refundable deposits.

Before I realized it, I was sitting in front of the church.

Perfect Timing, I said to myself because Tracey pulled up right beside me.

Oh, good. Now I don't have to walk in alone.

I smiled and waved to her as she slid into the parking spot and straightened her wheel. I checked my hair and applied some lip-gloss.

I took a well-needed and distinctively deep breath as I gave myself a reassuring smile in my car visor mirror. I grabbed my purse and Bible and prepared to exit my car.

Before I did, I gave myself a quick pep talk: *Okay, you can do this. God is waiting*, I told myself.

I got out of the car and came around to Tracey's driver side backseat door and waited for her to gather herself together so that we could enter the church building together.

There is strength in numbers, I said to myself.

By the time I looked up again, she was getting out of the car with a great big smile on her face.

"Good morning," she smiled and sang to me.

"You seem particularly chipper this morning," I said, not nearly as enthusiastically as she had to me.

"I just know that God is going to do something amazing today." She winked at me as she ushered me into the church foyer.

"Okay, here it goes," I said loud enough for only God and I to hear and put on my best smile.

"Good morning," one of the greeters said as we crossed the threshold and were preparing to enter the sanctuary. I braced myself.

"Is this your first visit?" She smiled at me. "Welcome to our church." She offered me a hug.

I nodded "yes" and gave her another one of my best smiles. I figured if I looked like I belonged here, no one would find me out.

"Welcome, welcome. We are blessed that you chose to worship with us today. Here is a welcome packet. Please, before you leave today, fill out the guest card inside of your packet and put it in this mailbox." She finished as she pointed to the maple colored mailbox just outside of the sanctuary sitting on a birch colored counter.

"Okay, thank you," I said.

"Come on," Tracey said and grabbed my arm to find a seat in the sanctuary. We made our home in the third row center of the emerald green and gold well-decorated sanctuary. I must say, since you only get one chance to make a first impression, the church made an amazing one.

As we prepared to sit, members came over to say hello and welcome me. We got there just before praise and worship was scheduled to begin so there was not a lot of time for chatting before the music started.

At 10:30 on the dot, every person was in place and the praise team, which included the Pastor and First Lady, was singing and preparing to usher in God's presence. I was impressed. In all my years of church, I had never seen one when the Pastor was in the sanctuary at the start of the service! Typically, they came in about a half an hour or so later after the service started with an entourage the size of the Village People.

Immediately, I took note of this little church that had been given its name based on the simplicity of a relationship with Christ. As a Christian, your purpose is to praise Him, worship Him and read His Word. This church was already showing me that they truly did things in decency and order. I only glanced around at the other members for a moment before I decided to focus on my reason for being there and closed my eyes.

Lord, I need You now. I am here today to hear a word from You, Lord. I need to know which way to go. I need to know how to pick up the pieces of my shattered life and get my life together. I need Your help to find out who I am. I have tried it my way. I have lost so much. I gave Trenton everything I had and now I am empty. I want so desperately to be loved and I need You to show me how. I know that You allowed things to happen the way they did. For that, I thank You. You knew that I was not strong enough to make that decision myself so You did it for me. I knew a long time ago that Trenton was not the man for me but I was so weak that I kept living the lie. I know that I owe you so much for all that You have done for me. Saving me from myself has made a big difference and even though I am low in spirit now, I know that I am a victor and not a victim. I thank You. Lord, I thank You. Now, strengthen me Lord. That is the only way that I can survive. I pray this prayer in Jesus' name, amen. I wept deeply as I released it all to God.

I heard the words of the song playing and reflected inwardly as I prepared myself to surrender all to the Lord.

I felt my face getting hot and I felt myself shifting in my place. I was moved by the fact that God had brought me safely to this place. As I thought about how He loved me in spite of myself, I started to scream at the top of my lungs. It was like I was having an out of body experience. I was so moved with a need to express my thanks to the Lord. I swayed back and forth but something told me to stop.

You are making a fool of yourself, the voice said. *You should just stop; you look ridiculous. People know.*

Nonetheless, the connection was broken and I opened my eyes and looked around. No one was paying me any attention so I just composed myself, grabbed the tissues that were left on my seat and sat down. I decided that I would just enjoy the music from my seat and wait for the Pastor to preach his sermon. I think they sang three more songs before the church erupted in praise.

Every way I turned, there was someone having a "personal spiritual fit." There was dancing, stomping, yelling and all the while there were smiles across their faces. They appeared to be elated that they were in the presence of the Lord. This activity looked commonplace and everyone appeared to be concerned about one thing: praising God.

As I listened to the song being played, the psalmist said that God was concerned about the condition of my heart. What was the condition of my heart? *Broken, confused, lonely, desperate, desolate and fearful*, I thought to myself.

I didn't know what God could do to help me since He knew the condition of my heart. Somehow I felt that because my heart was heavy, He wouldn't help me.

As I thought that, something told me, *don't believe that. I am here to restore the years you have sown in tears. In order to reap joy, you have to go through something. You have sown in tears and I am ready to restore you.*

Somehow I knew that my earlier thoughts of defeat and despair were just the enemy trying to keep me from getting the deliverance I needed to move on. I was confident that the Lord was speaking to me right then.

I tried to settle myself as the voice spoke softly to me again. *I am here for you. I promised to never leave or forsake you. Trust me. Surrender your will to me and I will give you rest.* Again I smiled, confident that I was hearing God speak.

I suddenly felt so comfortable in this place. I closed my eyes and just let the music minister to me. "Lord, I've got to worship You. Everything's going to be all right." I said to myself over the music. I could sense that I was going to be fine.

It was evident that the spirit of the Lord was in this church. That still small voice whispered assuredly to me, *everything's going to be all right. Just trust and believe in Me. I am not a man that I should lie. You can trust Me. I will not hurt you like Trenton has done. I will love you like you deserve to be loved. You have put your confidence in man instead of trusting in Me. Read My Word. I made it clear in Psalm 118:8 that trust in Me is what will bring you the ultimate gift: love. The love that you seek is right here in My arms. Come wholly, fully and honestly into My presence and I will love you. I already do.*

The tears poured from the windows of my soul as I listened to the voice tell me exactly what was wrong with me. I had always put my confidence in man. I had always expected that a man was the answer to my lonely cries and prayers but here I clearly heard God telling me to trust in Him and He would give me the love I desired.

But how could I trust in Him to love me when I was lonely at night? I was still trying to assess all that was going on in my confused and slightly crowded mind when I heard the Pastor speak.

"Praise the Lord." The Pastor took his place at the podium. "Does anybody have a reason to praise the Lord this morning? Hallelujah. Come on, I know you've got a reason to praise Him." I looked around, hands were lifted up and mouths were full of praise.

"I'm going to be before you for only a little while this morning, church. I have a Word from the Lord that has been sitting in my spirit since Wednesday. I have been praying over this Word all week long and now God has told me to release it. Those who need to receive of this Word are among us. Praise Your name, oh God. Turn with me if you will to Psalm 32."

I looked around the sanctuary, I saw everyone enthusiastically turning in their Bibles. I knew this passage. I'd been reading it all week long.

"We are going to be looking specifically at verses ten and eleven but I encourage you to read the entire Psalm. Don't worry, church. It's a short one," he chuckled. "Here we have a Psalm of David, a man after God's own heart. I want to preach to you today from the subject of Rejoice."

I perked up when he said he would be preaching from Psalm 32. And when he said verses ten and eleven, I really went crazy on the inside. My stomach would have come out of my mouth had my mouth been open. That was the exact passage that God had sent me to on Wednesday evening when I was sitting in my car in the Comcast parking lot. I couldn't believe that God would tell this Pastor to preach the same exact thing that he told me to read on Wednesday.

And I know I heard the Pastor say that he had received that Word on Wednesday.

Did the Pastor know what happened to me? I wondered to myself. *Did God tell him because He knew that I would be in this church today to hear confirmation of the words that He himself had given me to make sure that I got the message*? I continued my personal inquisition.

Realizing that I was missing key components of the message that I truly felt was being preached for me, I decided to turn my thoughts off so that I could focus on what this man of God had to say.

"Let me read the verses to you church, here David writes in verse ten 'many sorrows shall be to the wicked: but he that trusteth in the Lord, mercy shall compass him about.' There is someone here today with many sorrows. Trust in the Lord, that's what God's Word says. Trust in the Lord. Verse eleven: Be glad in the Lord, and rejoice. There's that word church. Be glad in the Lord, and rejoice, ye righteous: and shout for joy, all ye that are upright in heart.'" He had repeated that last verse for effect.

"You may have many sorrows," he continued "but if you trust in the Lord, you will rejoice. The Bible says Rejoice. God is not a man that He should lie. If He said you would rejoice, you will rejoice. I am not sure who exactly this is for but God is telling me to let you know that your sorrows are over. Oh, somebody ought to rejoice over that. Your sorrows are over!"

With that, the Pastor lost it. He backed up from the podium and started to dance and praise the Lord. Right on cue, the First Lady started the "shouting music" so that he could get his praise on. He was praising God for me; I just knew that he was.

I couldn't believe God. After all that I had done, after all the wrong, the hurt, the pain and embarrassment that I am sure my behavior had caused Him, He was still blessing me. And even though I didn't feel that my sorrows were over right then, I received that they were coming to an end.

I turned to Tracey and mouthed, "thank you." She nodded in my direction, acknowledging my sentiment.

Suddenly, I was so overwhelmed with a desire to get up off my feet and dance for the Lord. And I did. I got caught up in the music and bucked my way out of my shoes and knocked over a few chairs along the way. But I didn't care, I felt free. The God that loved me had sent a special message to me through this house because He knew before I did that I would be in this exact situation and have need for reassurance that He had my back.

I serve an Incredible God.

After the praise break, the Pastor continued his sermon and called for prayer.

"I'm going to do something different today and we are going to have our altar call in the middle of the message. Someone here is in need of prayer right now. Your heart is heavy. You've come here hoping that God would reveal himself to you. God wants to love you and give you exactly what you've been seeking in man. Psalm 118:8 makes it clear to us that it is better to trust in the Lord than to put confidence in man. He wanted me to tell you again. He said that He has told you, He even told you today during this service, but you still doubt Him and His power to love you like you deserve to be loved. If you are ready to rejoice and leave your sorrows behind, form a line right in the center aisle so that I can pray for you."

I turned around to see if anyone was moving. No one moved. I heard the gentle voice whisper, "go." I fidgeted in my seat. I was too afraid that they would know the embarrassment that I felt if I got up. I don't know why though, that is why I had come, to hear from the Lord. I don't know why I was so afraid.

The voice got a little louder "Go." I continued to sit, as if I didn't know He was talking to me. I heard Him as clear as day but I wanted to pretend like nothing was happening in my life that forced my need to rejoice and leave my sorrows behind. Tears started to fall as I tried to pretend like He was not talking to me.

This time, the voice was very loud and piercing in my ear. "GO!"

Startled, I shifted in my seat and stood by accident.

The Pastor looked up and said "God bless you, please come. I have been waiting for you."

Chapter 21

So the king asked me, "Why does your face look so sad when you are not ill?" This can be nothing but sadness of heart.

Nehemiah 2:2

I was beginning to feel better. I was still sad from time to time and I was so lonely, but it wasn't as bad as it had been. By this time, everyone close to me was aware of the news. I was so sick of hearing people say, "That dog!" or "Oh, no. I am so sorry for you." I could scream.

All the extra time away from civilization did not help, either. I had been shut up in my house trying to "deTrentoninize" it and all that extra heartache was wearing on me. Each article of clothing that belonged to him or that I had worn in the past three years brought back a memory. Every gift that he had given me had a tremendous story. And then there was the ring. I did not give it back. I said that I would keep it as a reminder not to allow myself to make the same mistake twice: I did not want to allow any man to dictate my life's course.

I did want to continue to love and love fully with a heart of trust. With God in my life, I felt assured that the next man would have my best interests at the forefront of his mind simply because I knew better for myself.

During this time, I learned that I didn't have to have a man to complete me; that was a misconception. In order to walk into that realization, I had to get to a place of quiet and isolation so that I, more importantly God, could deal with me. I had to face some harsh realities about myself so that I could leave the past behind and move forward.

As I spent time getting to know myself, I was also detoxifying my existence from the bondage of my past. I had been bound by being molested. I had been bound by my mother's incarceration. I was shackled to the fact that my dad never told me he loved me. My brothers and sisters constant tormenting "you think you are better than us" detained me. Replaying that phone conversation that my stepmother had with her mother when she said, "I wish they weren't here" kept my mind bogged down with the fact that I was not enough. I was a prisoner because I felt like I was unlike anyone else in the whole world. I had gotten out that old lock box of secrets and I was getting delivered from my past.

Those secrets would never haunt me again.

My solitary confinement was necessary to truly encapsulate my issues and remove them from my mind. My mind had become the devil's playground and I did not like that. He taunted me and accused me of terrible things. He played on my weaknesses, especially how I felt about myself and tried to kill me. He gave me thoughts of ending my life, which had been selected by God to bless others.

Once all the confusion was gone, I could allow God to truly move into my heart. Since God does not operate in confusion, all confusion had to be displaced before he would manifest His presence in my life. I realized that each part of this process was very necessary. He had given me little nuggets along the way to let me know that He wanted to love me.

The time spent away from everyone allowed me to do that. I knew that I had to do it alone, without anyone else's help. The only other consultants on this matter of grave importance were Char, my therapist, my daily journal and God.

Between the four of us, I started to love myself. I realized that what I had pretended all those years was true. I realized that I was different and different was okay. Different was a blessing. I walked into my greatness and embraced the good things that I believed about me. I realized that I was a great person.

Looking back over the relationship I had with Trenton taught me that I needed to love myself first and foremost. If I did not, I would never get the love and respect that I deserved to feel from my partner. Trenton walked over me because I let him. I didn't hold myself in high enough regard to warrant him to treat me differently. Self-love would only come to me by the way of my Father who lived in Heaven. Through Christ, I could experience the kind of love that never failed.

As far as a man loving me, I would decide to wait patiently for God to send me the man who would deserve to have my whole heart as I learned that His Word was clear when in Proverbs 18:22 He says *He who findeth a wife finds a good thing and obtains favor from the Lord.* My time apart taught me that I am a good thing. I am worth the wait. I am the key to someone's favor.

It was getting easier to say his name without the flood coming. I almost felt like, "Trenton who?" I say almost because from time to time, I would feel come kind of way.

Truthfully Trenton had been a big part of my life. It was because of him that I was now in a place of contentment, working my way up to a place of joy. I couldn't change the past but I could commandeer the future. I held the power to control my mind, body and spirit all along. I really owe Trenton a great big "thank you," as his mistake catapulted me into my destiny.

I loudly reminded myself, "That which does not kill us makes us stronger." I don't know if in all cases that statement is true, but in my case, it sure enough was.

I was stronger because of my journey. My arrival at this destination in my life would not have been possible without the grace and mercy of my Lord and Savior, Jesus Christ.

I heard the Lord say, *life and death lies in the power of your tongue. Speak life and you shall live. Remember that fear is just false evidence appearing real. Everything you want is on the other side of your fears. My child, know that fear and faith cannot occupy the same place. Trust Me and I promise you that joy will walk ahead of you all the days of your life.*

Chapter 22

Since you have kept my command to endure patiently, I will also keep you from the hour of trial that is going to come upon the whole world to test those who live on earth. Revelation 3:10

I was in a particularly good mood that Tuesday afternoon when I left work. The day had been peaceful and serene. With my boss out of the office, I was able to focus and really get some work done. I was even able to leave a little earlier to take in some of the beautiful day that I got a taste of at lunch.

As I drove home, I looked at the sun as it shone brightly. I could hear the birds singing their favorite song. The day of perfection was moderately temperate and I was just so glad to be taking it all in.

When I got home and got the mail, there was an ivory colored linen envelope that looked a little suspect. There was no return address and I didn't recognize the handwriting that had written my name and address. I didn't hesitate to open it. I pulled the corner and revealed the type-faced letter inside. Still a little perplexed, I opened the letter.

I immediately realized it was from Trenton. I glanced down to the body of the letter.

I knew that if I called you, you would hang up on me so I figured that I could get my thoughts out uninterrupted in writing, so here it goes:

When we met all those years ago, I knew that you were the woman who would change my life. From that first day at the firm, your smile pierced my heart and I was never the same. I made it my business to get your attention and it seemed that you were not interested in me like I was interested in you. I kept praying to God that you would notice me and want to share the same time and space as I. I prayed for you everyday. I dreamt of you each night. You were the first thought on my mind as each new day dawned.

I knew that I had found my ruby, my virtuous woman and I was so elated. When you stayed by my side when I quit my good job to follow my dream, I knew that God had truly blessed me with the woman that I had prayed for. When I took you home to meet my family and you fit right in, I rejoiced over you inwardly. You may never know how much I loved you but I did. In fact, I still do.

At night, when you were asleep, I use to watch you and pray that God would cover you in His love. I knew that you were wounded and I wanted so desperately to save you. I knew that your family had abandoned and not loved you the way that you needed and deserved to be loved and I wanted so badly to offer you the love that you craved as a result of never getting loved right as a child.

When you got pregnant, I lost it. I freaked out. I looked at your face, so excited, so in love and I knew that you wanted our child more than anything in the world. I didn't know how I, this misfit, who was killing his own life was going to be able to take care of another one. I did something unspeakable. I asked you, the woman I loved, to abort our child. I asked you to kill a child that we conceived in the truest and purest love. I couldn't be the man you needed me to be so I demanded that you choose me over our unborn child.

Bottom line, I was selfish. I am so sorry that I hurt you. I have never forgiven myself for making you have that abortion. Will you please forgive me? I was selfish and insensitive to your feelings. All you did was love me and I refused to let you into my whole world.

I think that was the first nail that I slid into the coffin of our relationship. Although I prayed for you to come into my life, once I was granted the blessing, I didn't know how to take care of it. I misused the gift God gave me and I allowed the enemy to take it away from me as the devil used Constance to take me off course. After you got rid of our child, I immediately felt horrible and embarrassed. I knew that you did it out of love for me but I hated myself for making you make that choice. I know that it had to be dreadful for you to do that. For what it is worth, I am so sorry.

I don't know if I loved you as much as you had to love me to put up with my mess over the years. I know that you may never forgive me for making you choose. The fact that you chose me over our unborn child meant that you really loved me. After that point, I had no idea how to live up to the love that you had displayed for me so instead I took it out on you, treating you bad, being insensitive, ignoring you, getting drunk and doing terrible things to you to your knowledge and unbeknownst to you. I started blaming everything and everyone except the one responsible for your misery: me.

When you started going to therapy to get help from someone else instead of talking to me about our problems, I felt emasculated. When you stopped being affectionate towards me, I died a little on the inside. Not the fact that we stopped being intimate, but the fact that I couldn't even touch your cheek without you having to do your best to disguise the contempt in your heart for me. I could see it. I knew that you hated me for what I had done to you. Without realizing it, I had become your father who never told you that he loved you. I had become the man who misused his power of influence over you and took advantage of your innocence. I knew deep down that it was only a matter of time before we were through. I told myself that it was over. It was over in my heart.

I still don't understand why you stayed so much longer after you started to hate me. I continued to beat myself up inwardly instead of confiding in you. I know now that my solitary complaining and inward dealing with the issues ruined any chances of survival for us. When it came right down to it, I did not deserve you. You are too good and deserve to be loved entirely and wholly by a good man. I was not a good man. I misused my power and created emptiness inside you that I will never forgive myself for.

When Constance started coming on to me, I figured that you had figured out what a coward I was and it was only a matter of time before you left me. I knew that you were aware of her growing presence in my life. I cannot even give you a plausible excuse as to why she was even there. I could blame it on the devil. But I need to take ownership and tell you that I was not thinking with my brain. The thinking that I was doing was coming from a different place entirely.

I proposed to you because I felt that I owed you a better life since I made you kill our child. But I was a failure and I couldn't give you the life you deserved. So I did something that I never thought I would ever do anyone, least of all you, I cheated and I carelessly made a baby with someone else. The baby that was supposed to have been ours, securing our future, was now a mistake made with a woman I didn't love, trust or couldn't even stand the sight of. You were right about her from the start but as a man with a wounded sense of pride, she played on my weaknesses and made me feel powerful and needed. That is not an excuse for what I did to you, it is just the truth of the matter.

I know that if you had that baby, we would be happily married in a few months. I hate myself for what I have done to you. I cried myself to sleep for nights after I realized that I had become one of them. I had always promised myself that I would never be like those men who ran other women for years but I did, I became one in the same.

For what it's worth, I do love you. I do want to marry you. I know now more than ever that God picked you for me. But I also know 'to whom much is given, much is required." God gave you to me. I know that for sure as I write this letter. The problem is that I forgot it in the heat of the moment when I made a stupid mistake and gave in to her desires, gave in to my own. I forgot it when I made horrible choices that would haunt me later in my life. Had I stayed true to us, we would be married and granted another chance at having a family. But I blew it. I am so sorry.

I know now more than ever that I messed it up. I know that I may never realize my dream of loving you as my wife but know that forever a piece of my heart will always belong to you.

If for any reason you change your mind about me and want to grant me another chance, please do not hesitate to call me. I will be waiting. I will always love you and I am forever in your debt for all that you did for me. You are truly an amazing woman. I wish things were different. I am kicking myself that I missed out on my Heaven here on earth.

Yours forever and eternally sorry,
Trenton

P.S. Here is the money I owe you. I hope that it eases the pain in some way.

By the time I was finished reading the letter, I was smiling. I had started out crying but by the end of the letter, a smile blanketed my face. It was over. I finally felt like I could get past the fact that I had chosen him over my child. I had made a bad choice; a choice that today I was now remembering had cost me everything. But I had also gained a lot as a result of that choice. I had forgiven myself and God had tossed it into the sea a long time ago. I mentally lit a candle in remembrance of our relationship and then I moved on.

I was also glad to get that $2,800.00 check that he'd enclosed.

Once inside my house, I found solace in the peaceful colors adorning my walls. The soft rose and rich purple welcomed me home, a place where I felt serenity. I looked up at the wall where my favorite painting "God's Angels" hung. The black dancing angels perfectly centered on the soft rose wall in hues of pink, purple, gold and light brown made me smile. Ribbons of white enveloped each angel.

At the end of the day, I had to thank Trenton. I may have never realized my destiny had he and Constance not pushed me into thinking a different thought and becoming a different person. I realized that I had to go through this to get to the other side of my destiny. Although it was difficult, it was worth it. No pain, no gain.

As the angels smiled at me, the Holy Spirit whispered *take comfort in my presence. I am here for you. I will never leave you. Everything is all right. Trust Me.*

I found a place on the ecru colored Italian leather sofa. As I sat down, I slid back in comfort allowing the sofa to overwhelm me. I could feel God's tender warmth stir my spirit and soothe my soul.

"I trust You Lord," I shouted aloud.

That letter represented the past. *The past is behind me, I am moving on, my best days are ahead of me*, I thought to myself.

I took a deep breath and heard God say, *you've got it, My child. Forget what is behind you, press toward the mark for My calling, the calling of love. I love you. I am here. I am the one you need. Stop allowing man to influence what you will become. I have made you in My image. Believe that you can be whole if you allow Me to work in and through you. I want to make you complete in Me.*

Chapter 23

Shout and be glad, o Daughter of Zion. For I am coming, and I will live among you, declares the Lord.

Zechariah 2:10

Even though it had been quite some time since Trenton and I broke up, it was still so hard for me to get use to being single again. There were times when I had some low moments. Part of me still feared being left alone and here I was, alone again.

I still wanted more than ever to have the security of love in my life and I was not feeling the love. My friends tried to comfort me, but what I needed, they couldn't give me. I knew I only had to look to the hills to find my help but something, despite the evidence that love did exist for me, was still holding me back from walking full force into Christ's arms.

I wasn't sure exactly what was holding me back, but I had to find out. It was the key to securing my future. I had been in therapy with Char for some time now and I realized that I had repressed a lot of stuff that kept me bound despite my desire to be free to love myself and serve the Lord.

I told myself that I was over those issues but they were still there. God couldn't get into the cracks and crevices of my soul because the memories of my life were still blocking the path that He wanted to take. But week-by-week a little more of my heart became exposed to the agape love of Christ. It was weird; I wanted Him; but I was taking my sweet time walking the short distance into His loving arms. Although I had a true desire to live right, I still had a little resistance to truly allowing God to work in me.

Inwardly I wondered, w*hy couldn't I surrender to You totally Lord*?

I really wanted to give God my all. I started attending weekly Bible study so that I could learn the Word for myself. I had to know God for myself; a personal relationship would be the key to my salvation.

My personal relationship with Christ would sustain me and help to ensure that I did not put my confidence in any man. I started to learn more scriptures and kept a running tab of the ones that personally ministered to me and gave me hope that one day, God would be proud to have me in His Kingdom.

I am proud to have you now, My child. I heard Him tell me.

I started to develop a fire for the Lord. I felt like Jeremiah, fire was shut up in my bones when I thought of God's goodness and grace.

I remembered back to the time as a child when my mom told me that God had a special job for me in His Kingdom. I had been told on several occasions that God had placed a special anointing on my life. I remembered how it had gone over my head that day, but now, I knew that it was time for me step up to God's plate so that He could hit a home run in my life.

I was slowly getting rid of "my demons" and anger with the help of the Holy Spirit. Each week, you would find me rearranging the chairs with a wild praise for God. My praise was wild because I was still stifled and afraid of what God wanted to do in me. I knew that He had something big planned for my life and it scared me. I had never been one of those, "if You can use anything Lord, You can use me" people. The thought of standing up to be counted for Christ still had me weak at the knees.

At church each Sunday, God's presence would rest in my bosom but I wouldn't let it loose and so eventually God would come in and take His praise, which sent me off into a wild fit. It was complete with screaming, crying, jumping, dancing and oh, kicking off my shoes. And that happened every week.

Admittedly, I was still angry about so many things that had happened in my past. I was getting over it but it sounds a lot easier than it is when people say "let go and let God." I was realizing that in order for God to become love for me, I had to let it all go. I had thought that I had let stuff go, but I had just hidden my issues, fears and concerns way back in the deep crevices of my heart.

Where the spirit of the Lord is, there is liberty; His word spoke to my heart.

But why couldn't I press forward? I asked myself.

I heard God say, *release it all to me*.

I wasn't entirely sure what He meant because I had given Him my heart. I prayed the prayer of commitment and surrendered to His will for me. *Hadn't I*?

Chapter 24

To open their eyes and turn them from darkness to light, and from the power of Satan to God, so that they may receive forgiveness of sins and a place among those who are sanctified by faith in me.

Acts 26:18

I was leaving the mall on a Wednesday evening as my phone rang. Instinctively, I looked down to see who it was. I did not recognize the number, but something told me that it was Trenton. It had been a year and a half since we had spoken.

Why was he calling me, now? I thought to myself.

I couldn't decide if I wanted to answer the phone or not. So I let it go to voicemail. Once my phone signaled that I had a voicemail, I decided to check it.

I had been right; it was Trenton. I don't know how I knew it had to be him but somehow it just seemed like it had to be. I was happy. I was more confident than ever and I loved life and myself, so of course the enemy would try to throw a monkey wrench in my joy. It was weird, I didn't want to talk to him and I felt confident in my stance but I wanted to know why after all this time he was calling me. He had paid me back for the loan as well as all of the wedding deposit money so the way I saw it, there was no reason for us to talk about anything ever again.

I was in a good place. My faith was strong and my life was settled. I was comfortable in my skin and I was finally at a place where I did not blame the past for my actions or the choices that I made at that time in my life. The past was just that, the past. Wasn't it?

I thought about what his voicemail said again. "Hey. It's Trenton. I know you are wondering why I am calling you. I need to talk to you. I was hoping that maybe we could meet for lunch. Anyway, give me a call when you get a chance. You have my number I hope but I will leave it again just in case. I will be waiting. Goodbye."

"Yes, he would." I said out loud.

I wasn't sure how I felt about him wanting to talk to me. I decided to take it to the Lord in prayer. If God said it was okay, then we would talk.

I got to my car and put my purchases on the back seat.

Why does he want to talk to me? I thought to myself again as I shut the back door and climbed into the driver's seat.

"Let it go." I told myself.

But I couldn't. I decided right then and there to pray before I moved my car from that spot in front of Macy's.

Dear Lord, first and foremost I want to thank You not because of what You've done, but because of who You are. You are my joy and my strength. I need You now Lord. I thank You for Your love and guidance. I thank You for Your spirit. Thank You for showing me how to believe in myself. Thank You for helping me to love myself. I know that You heard the message that Trenton left me. I don't know what to do Lord. I need Your wisdom. My heart says to never call him back. I don't care what he wants. I am finally in a good place where I love myself. I know that there is a reason that he is calling me now. The devil knows that I am doing better, much better. He knows that I am getting stronger everyday. And he is trying to take me off course. Somehow, he has looked into my future and he knows that You are doing an incredible work in me and he wants to stir the pot. I rebuke the devil right now in the name of Jesus. Calm my flesh, Lord. Help me to think with a clear head and focus on You and Your will for my life. I trust You to tell me what to do Lord. I trust You. I pray this prayer in Jesus' name, amen.

Then I got quiet and waited for God to speak. I decided to turn on my car so that I could listen to a gospel compilation CD of slow praise and worship songs. It played softly and filled the car with serenity. I closed my eyes, put my head back on the headrest and waited for God to speak. I knew that He would.

I sang along lightly to the instrumental music. "He is here. God is here. Let Your presence feel this place and all my fears erase. God is here to take away the pain."

I was sitting and patiently waiting for His Shekinah Glory to fill my spirit when suddenly His voice spoke softly and calmly to me.

You are fearfully and wonderfully made in My image. I am so proud of the progress that you have made in your heart, where I reside and want to live forever. Do not be afraid to reach out to Trenton; he needs closure. The fact that he wants to talk to you is about him, not you. You can allow him to speak his peace but make sure that you are comfortable. Trust your judgment. Don't do anything that you don't feel comfortable with but allow him to get the closure he needs. I love you and I will always be with you. I will never leave you.

I replayed God's message in my head as I drove the short distance to Bible study. After we were finished our lesson,

I asked for a few minutes of my Pastor's time just to run this scenario by him. As I listened to him say exactly what God had shared with me earlier that day, I knew confidently that I could hear the Lord. I left Bible study elated. I was so pumped that I had been able to get quiet and hear the Lord speak to me.

"Thank You, Lord." I shouted as I drove home. "Thank You God for Your provision and the promises in Your Word. You told me that as Your child I would know Your voice. I am so thankful to You that I am Your child. Thank you Jesus. Hallelujah. Bless Your name God."

Once I got home and got settled, I decided to call Trenton back. I had to listen to the message again to get the phone number he wanted me to reach out to him on. As I replayed the message and listened to his voice, I could hear fear in his voice. I could just see him now, shaking as he tried to figure out what he would say if I actually answered the phone when he had called.

I dialed the number and it rang and then went to voicemail so I left a message.

"Hi Trenton, you know who this is. I'm returning your call. I am not interested in having lunch with you but if you would like to talk, you may call me tomorrow evening after 6 pm. I will be available until 7:30 pm. If that works for you, I will talk to you then. Thanks."

With that, I put a movie in the DVD player, popped some popcorn and settled into my bed. I decided to watch a movie until it was watching me.

Chapter 25

Therefore, my brothers, I want you to know that through Jesus the forgiveness of sins is proclaimed to you.

Acts 13:38

My phone rang at exactly 6 pm the following night. It was Trenton. I answered on the second ring.

"Hello."

"Um, hi. It's Trenton." He was shaken. His voice was an octave higher than I remembered.

"Hey." I said in a monotone voice. "You know, I always wondered what I would say to you when given the chance. But as I thought about this conversation today, I decided that I was just going to pray for you and my own strength instead."

I paused to let what I said sink in.

"What can I do for you?" There was no reason for small talk. I wanted to cut to the chase.

"Um, how are you?" He stammered.

"I am well, thanks for asking." I didn't return the question.

"Well, uh, I wanted to call you and just see how you uh were doing. It's been a long time. Uh, I have never stopped thinking about you."

He paused as if he were waiting for me to say something. I said nothing. I liked the idea of the uncertainty messing with him a little.

Then he continued, "Uh, I wanted to ask for your forgiveness for what I did to you back then." His voice got lower, like he was embarrassed.

He should be.

"Yeah, I know you haven't stopped thinking about me. I still get your greeting cards every month."

"I am glad that you read them."

"Who said anything about reading them? I said I get them when they come. They are unopened. You can have them back if you'd like."

"No, they are for you."

"Trenton, seriously, I have forgiven you, for *everything*. That is the only way that I could move on and allow God to love me. I couldn't profess to love Him but harbor hate for you. I never hated you; I hated what you did to me."

"I am so sorry. Did you get my letter?"

"Yes, I did."

"But you never said anything."

"There was no need to. Like I said, I have forgiven you."

"Good. I am glad to hear that. Uh, I really want to…"

I cut him off. "There is no need to say anything else. Just let it go. I wish you the best and I hope that you get exactly what God has for you."

"Please just let me finish. It took me so much to build up the nerve to even call you. I know you don't owe me anything, but please let me speak my peace."

"Okay."

"I just wish you could give me a second chance, I still love you. I know that I messed up but I know that if given a chance, I could really make you happy." He paused.

I started to say something but then he finished his thought, "If not, maybe we could at least part as friends."

"Don't you have a girlfriend?" I had heard through the grapevine that he was dating an attorney.

"If given the chance to make things right with you, I would make myself available."

I shook my head. This fool and the poor attorney who was fool enough to date him. Some things never change. It had been almost two years.

"I am sorry but that is not an option. I have no desire to have anything to do with you. I have forgiven you. But it's over for me. Friendships and relationships are based on trust and I am sorry but I do not trust you and I could never find myself in a place where I could go there with you ever again. And besides I don't want you. You are the past. I am focused on my future."

"Ouch." He said then took a deep breath. "I guess I have to respect that."

"Life is all about realizing your mistakes and learning from them. There are very few chances to do things over."

"Why does it have to be that way?"

"I don't trust you."

"But it's been years, I have changed."

"I hope that you have."

"But you're not buying it?"

"Not at all."

"I guess I deserve that."

"Yes, you do. Wait, I owe you a great big thank you. Had it not been for you, I would have never gotten to love myself and I definitely would not have truly met Jesus. So thank you. I wish you well in life. So take care. Goodbye."

"Come on, before you hang up, how have you been?"

"Are you serious?"

"Yeah, how have you been?"

"Trenton, I am not interested in catching up with you. If you don't have anything else to say that is pertinent, I am going to go. Take care of yourself." I hung up the phone.

Go ahead with your bad self, I smiled inwardly.

I looked up and gave God a smile from my heart. *Thank You, Lord.* It was finished.

I was in love under new management.

It had been a long time coming that Trenton would want to have a conversation about what had happened in the past and I thanked the Lord that enough time had passed for me to be able to handle the conversation like an adult. I will be honest with you, for a long time I was angry. I was mad because I felt like I had given him everything I had and he just took it. But one thing I know for sure is that when you let God into your heart, he softens it and helps you to find forgiveness for those things, situations and people who meant you harm. Trenton knew what he was doing and he knew that by doing it he would ruin any chances then or in the future for us to be friends.

I was able to forgive him and move on with my life but act as if it never happened, child please! I am not the one for that.

Chapter 26

So I say, live by the Spirit and you will not gratify the desires of the sinful nature. For the sinful nature desires what is contrary to the Spirit and the Spirit what is contrary to the sinful nature. They are in conflict with each other so that you do not do what you want. But if you are led by the Spirit, you are not under the law. The acts of the sinful nature are obvious: adultery, fornication, eagerness for lustful pleasure, idolatry, witchcraft, hatred, discord, jealousy, fits of rage, selfish ambition, dissensions, factions, envy, drunkenness, orgies, and the like. I warn you, as I did before, that those who live like this will not inherit the kingdom of God.

Galatians 5:16- 21

Unfortunately, I learned that getting saved and renewing my relationship with Christ did not instantly make my issues, addictions and idiosyncrasies disappear. I was a bag of flesh and my flesh wanted to feel good again. I always felt loved when a man was close to me. Even though it often wasn't love, I associated that closeness with love and that had been enough for me. I still wanted to be loved in a way that only a man could love me.

I still wanted to be held at night and caressed with a slow hand. Trenton had ruined the thought of that for me for years but now, the floodgates were open as I reconnected with my sensuality. That had always been my vice and now that I was living for Christ, I think I wanted it even more.

It had been a long time since I had known a man and I just wanted a little taste.

I had made myself available to dating again. Two years had passed since the breakup with Trenton.

One night, I went to a mixer in Philly and I met a beautiful biracial man who just made me want to melt when I first laid eyes on him. His mother was Mediterranean and his dad was black. I got to know Aaron by talking to him that night and subsequently spending time together over the phone. Because he lived in Camden and I lived in Bear, we didn't get to spend a significant amount of time together.

Additionally, he was a medical student, which meant he had even less time to socialize. Anyway, things were progressing nicely and about three weeks after talking over the phone, on email, via instant messaging and text messaging, we agreed to have our first date. I went to Camden and we met at an Ethiopian restaurant.

I got my hair and nails done, bought a new summer sweater in a perfectly pale pink and prepared to make myself look amazing, just in case. I was fully into makeup by now and I took great care to prepare a natural but flawless look.

When I walked into the restaurant, he was standing there waiting for me with a dozen long-stemmed baby pink roses, as if he'd known that I'd be wearing that color that night. He smiled and the angels started to cry in Heaven. His teeth were so perfectly white.

I smiled just watching him. His green eyes sparkled with anticipation of a fun-filled night.

"Hey beautiful," he said and kissed me full on the lips.

Lord, have mercy on my soul! I sizzled and the party in my panties began. *I'd better brace myself*, I said inwardly.

"Hi, yourself." I managed to get out while blinking profusely trying to compose myself.

Had he just kissed me passionately at the beginning of our first date? I asked myself. He had.

"Turn around, let me look at you," he said in a confident and velvet voice. He took me by the hand and twirled me around ever so gently taking in my full beauty. I did look extra good.

When I was back facing him, I took a deep breath and drunk him in. He was six foot three; copper colored, with an athletic build and the most vibrant green eyes, curly jet-black hair and long, full, luscious lashes.

Yummy, I said under my breath. It was going to be a long night.

"So how was your drive?" Aaron asked me.

I smiled at him as he held my hand on the way to the table. "It was pretty good. Traffic moved steadily and I was here in no time."

He grabbed my hand and lowered his eyes and started to speak as he kissed my hand. "I'm glad you are here, my love."

I smiled. Was he for real? This guy was starting out on a good note. I was not expecting all of this. I loved to be shown affection and a guy who was not afraid of a public display got extra points.

"So, what's good here?" I smiled at him. It was so easy to smile at him. His facial features were so lovely. The eye candy made my sweet tooth hurt. I had to pinch myself to make sure that I was really in the presence of a man so fine. It had been a long time; although Trenton had a beautiful smile, he had absolutely nothing on Aaron.

"Well, I love most things but since you only eat chicken, I'd go for chicken sari. Wait, do you like hot and spicy food?" He winked at me as he asked that question.

"As a matter of fact, I do." I winked back.

"Okay, then, I would recommend that dish. We can also get some greens and wild rice to go with it. The only thing I want to point out is that we eat with our hands and this spongy bread. But I promise you; you'll love it."

The waiter appeared just in the nick of time as Aaron was coming in for another kiss. He placed our order. I loved that he took charge and ordered for us.

Once the waiter was gone, he made his second attempt to land his lips on my neck. He was successful. It was taking everything in me to hold it together and to resist the urge to blow this joint and go get busy.

Honestly, I wanted some badly. I knew I shouldn't but I did.

"So, tell me something about you that I don't know?" He smiled at me.

"Well," I began. "I am afraid of fire."

He touched my hand. "Really?"

"Yup. We had a fire when I was younger and ever since then, I have been deathly afraid. I won't even light a match."

"You are so beautiful."

I beamed at him. There was something about a man telling you that you are beautiful that made the whole world all right.

"Thank you. You are not so bad yourself." I winked at him.

He grabbed my hand and lightly stroked it as he ate and watched me intently. I was tingling just by watching the intensity in his eyes.

"So how does everything taste?"

"Everything tastes great," I said mid-bite.

"Good. Did I already tell you how beautiful you look tonight?"

"You did."

"When I saw you that night at the mixer, I kept saying to myself, 'I have to get to know that amazing woman.' Something about your essence spoke to me."

"Really?"

"Yes, beautiful. I love your dimples. I'd better be careful."

"Be careful? Why?"

"You may steal my heart if I am not paying attention."

Wow, he was a straight shooter too. I changed the subject.

"So, why medicine?"

"I have always wanted to be a doctor. I don't know. I think from way back when I use to watch Doogie Howser. I could totally see myself as an MD. Plus I look great in white." He winked at me.

I really enjoyed our meal. It was an interesting experience that I would have again and he was right, the food was amazing.

We finished dinner and exited the restaurant and headed for a reggae dance club and since it was a beautiful summer night, we decided to walk the few blocks to the club.

Once there, it was extremely crowded and very loud so we couldn't really talk much and the dancing was strictly bump and grind. As bad as I wanted it, I couldn't go out like that on the first date. So I decided that it was time to call it an evening. I knew that if I stayed, it would be harder to stay on track. We walked the few blocks back to our cars and I headed towards the New Jersey Turnpike South. I promised to call when I got home and as we said goodbye, he kissed me and I tingled all the way home.

Chapter 27

Therefore, I urge you, brothers, in view of God's mercy, to offer your bodies as living sacrifices, holy and pleasing to God – this is your spiritual act of worship.

Romans 12:1

When I got home, I didn't call Aaron right away. Instead, the Holy Spirit had spoken to me on the drive and sent me to Galatians 5:16-21. As I read those verses, I started crying. All this time, I had known that it wasn't right to have premarital relations but I never knew why. So I did it anyway. You know, ignorance is bliss. I thought that as long as you loved the person, it was acceptable. I mean you always heard old folks saying that physical intimacy was reserved for marriage but to be honest, I had no idea that the edict came from the Word of God. I know it sounds stupid but I never read the Word like I should have before I had a personal stake in getting to know God's Word.

At that very moment, I decided that if God said it then He would be able to sustain me and help me to become celibate. I knew that it would happen through no strength of my own. I knew that I would truly need God to help me along the way. I looked at the Word of God again and reread the last part of verse twenty-one out loud: "I warn you, as I did before, that those who live like this will not inherit the kingdom of God."

If God said it and I read it with my own eyes, it was enough for me. That was a powerful Word and I felt the desire get up and walk away as soon as I read the passage out loud. It was as if I had rebuked the devil, I guess truthfully I had done just that. At the name of Jesus, demons have to flee.

I decided after reading the Word and praying that I needed to have a conversation with Aaron right away. Once you know better, you are expected to do better and if we were going to continue to date, and I hoped that we would, he was going to have to respect my wishes to not have an intimate relationship.

I knew it would be hard and I fully anticipated that when I shared this with him, especially after such a steamy first date, he would be on his way out of my life. And, if Aaron couldn't handle my conditions then I would say good riddance to him.

I dialed his number and waited for him to answer.

He picked up on the third ring in a low and seductive tone.

Uh-oh, I said to myself.

He was starting with the sexy talk way too early in this conversation.

"Hello."

"Hey, I just wanted to let you know that I made it home. I actually got home about forty-five minutes ago but I had to handle an urgent matter as soon as I walked in the door. Were you sleeping?"

"No, I was waiting for you to call, mi amore." I could tell he was smiling as he answered. I loved his voice. It was so incredibly soothing.

"Oh, okay." I was waiting for the right moment to bring up our need to play it cool.

"I really like you. I can't wait to see you again. When can I see you again?" He sounded so excited and I have to admit, it was cute and I was flattered that a man wanted to be with me.

"Well I know week days are tough for you, right?"

"It depends, most days though I am in class, the lab or the library with my study group. Weekends are better."

"Okay, well, what time do you have classes? Could I meet you for lunch?"

"I guess but I'd like to spend some weekend time with you, too." He snickered kind of seductively.

I guess there's no time like the present.

"Remember when I told you that I was a born-again Christian?"

"Yeah."

"Well, what that means to me is that I am going to do my level best to live in accordance to God's Word. I have made it my business to strive for that each day. I am not perfect and will not ever be perfect but I want to do my best to make sure that He is pleased with me. My body is a living sacrifice to God."

"Okay." I could tell he was listening intently.

"I guess what I am trying to say is that I do like you too. But God's Word says that physical intimacy is reserved for marriage. I would like to get to know more about you but I am not interested in having a physically intimate relationship with you or anyone else." I paused. I have a tendency for just talking and talking.

"Really?" He sounded like he didn't believe what I just said.

"Yes, really."

"Okay. Even if two people really care about each other?"

"No matter the circumstances, physical intimacy before marriage is not God ordained." I responded with assurance.

"Wait, I go to church too and I never knew that. Is that in the Bible?" He was silent for a minute.

"It is." I wasn't about to have a Bible study with him. "That edict can be found in a few different places."

He paused for a few minutes. I assumed he was considering my proposition and weighing his options. I was bracing myself for him to say good-bye.

"Well, I understand. I respect your wishes. I have a question, though."

"Sure, what's up?"

"Does that mean that we can't kiss and hold hands? I am a very affectionate person."

"I know that. That is part of the reason why we are having this conversation tonight. No, it doesn't mean that we can't be affectionate, but because my goal is to remain celibate until marriage, the affectionate activity cannot take us down a path toward the bedroom. I just want to make sure that you have full disclosure now so that if things get heated, you don't act like you didn't know." I said confidently.

This was the first time ever in my life I was telling a man that there would be no physical intimacy and I meant it. I was choosing God over my favorite vice. I was determined to do right by God, finally. I felt confident and assured as I took my stand.

"I get it and I am okay with your beliefs as long as it means that we can hang out and spend time getting to know one another. It's all good, beautiful." He sounded sincere.

"Thanks for understanding Aaron."

"Anything for you, beautiful. So back to my original question, when will I see your beautiful face again?"

"How's Friday night?"

"Friday it is. I'll come to you this time. Let me check my schedule for the week and I will let you know when we can have lunch this week."

"All right, Aaron. Good night, I'll talk to you later. Sweet dreams."

Chapter 28

Submit yourselves then to God. Resist the devil and he will flee from you. James 4:7

Aaron made his way to Delaware that Friday evening. We decided on dinner and a movie; however, we never made it to the movie. After we ate, we stopped back to my house so that I could get a jacket and put on a pair of jeans. When I came back downstairs, Aaron was buck naked in my living room.

"What the…"

I started but he cut me off. It was a good thing, too. I was only on the cross with *Velcro* and it was about to be snatched off so I could give him a piece of my mind.

"Let me explain. I know that you said we would not have a physical relationship but I want you so bad. Just hanging out with you tonight and being so comfortable with you makes me feel really good about our future. I figured that if I let you see what you'd be getting, you would change your mind and we can make love."

I couldn't believe this fool. Make love? I didn't a bit more love him than the man in the moon. Granted, he looked magnificent; he knew good and well that I was not interested in going against the Word. We had that conversation not even five days ago. The way I saw it, there was not a man alive that I ever met that was worth losing the Kingdom for. So, Aaron had to go.

"Get dressed." I commanded in a stern voice. "I invited you into my home and you have disrespected me. I made it clear to you how I was rolling and you have blatantly disregarded that and my wishes. I have no desire to be with a man who does not value what I value. You clearly do not respect what is important to me. I will not settle for what you want to give me because I know that I deserve more. I am sorry but you need to leave and we," I glanced up at him and tried to focus on his face. "We are through." I finished.

I turned around and went back upstairs toward my bedroom. I sat on the steps completely out of view from him and waited for him to leave. Once I heard my front door close, I went to my bedroom window and peeked out to see his car backing out of my driveway.

"How dare he disrespect me in my own house?" I shouted.

"Thank You Lord for providing a way of escape as You promised in Your Word." I sighed then shrugged my shoulders as I added, "well, another one bites the dust."

I was so proud of myself. As I stood there taking in all that had just happened, I suddenly realized that it had been my fleshly desires that were preventing me from giving my all to Christ. I could give God my all excluding my sexuality because I had never reclaimed it from the faceless men of my past. Since I was seven, I had been fully aware of my sexuality. Because it had been misused against me, I continued to allow myself to use it as a pawn to get what I wanted and needed from men. Not loving myself enough to take a step back and realize the harm I was placing in my spirit by allowing men to come and go in my life, was defrauding my existence.

I allowed myself to believe that if I were intimate with a man, he would have to love me. He would have to give me what I craved and show me that love was all that matters. And although it is true that love is all that matters, there was no true love, no self love shared with those faceless men who clouded my past.

Right then and there, I got down on my knees and I prayed to the Lord out loud with a sincere heart:

"Dear Lord, I praise You. Thank You for being You. Thank You for saving me from myself. Thank You for showing me that I am valuable. Thank You for Your Word, which tells me that I am a virtuous woman with a price far above rubies. Thank You for Your love and showing me my worth. Thank You for removing the chains that had me bound to the sins of my past. Thank You for allowing me to forgive the men who used me and further contributed to my path of personal destruction. I thank You that I now realize that I had prevented You from giving me the right love, the agape love that would sustain me in the times of the storm. Thank You for filling my cup. Thank You for your "more than enough" mentality. Thank You for pouring into me throughout this trying time to show me that I am Your child. I am beautiful. Your Word validates me and I don't need any man to validate me. Thank You for gently wiping my tears as I discovered the past that kept me from fully loving and knowing You as my personal Lord and Savior."

"Thank You for waiting patiently while I continued to do the things that would keep me separated from You. Thank You for healing my sin-sick mind and showing me that I had a right to a life more abundant. Thank You for offering Your Word and Your Holy Spirit as a guide. Thank You for gentle correction and a Word that never fails. Thank You for giving me little nuggets of hope along the way to keep me encouraged and on the path to self-preservation. Thank You for placing in my spirit the will to forgive my parents for the wrongs I felt they had suffered me. Thank You for preparing me to love again with my whole heart. With Your help, I learned to stop holding others accountable for what happened to me and instead I focused on fixing the problem: me. I praise You Father. I love You, Father. I worship You Father. Hallelujah, Hallelujah. I praise You. I offer glory to Your name forever. In Jesus name I pray this prayer and thank You that it is finished. Amen."

When I got up with bruised knees, carpet fibers in my teeth and a tear stained face, I smiled. I was elated because I had not given in to Aaron and his beautiful nakedness, which had always been the one thing to which I couldn't say no. Although I once believed that I needed physical intimacy to get the love I desperately craved, I now realized that the love I desperately needed was the love of God and the love of self. I stood strong fully confident in the fact that I had taken a stand for God. I had taken a stand for myself. I was worth more. I was worth waiting for the love I deserved. I could boldly say that no more casual covenants would be made between the faceless men of my past and me. I finally believed that no fifteen minutes of pleasure were going to separate me from the love of Christ.

I turned on my stereo and let the music envelope me. Donald Lawrence and the Tri City Singers were singing *Restoring the Years*. I smiled and gave myself a big hug. God truly had restored the years that I had sown in tears. As they sang, "He's healing you, He's healing you," I realized that I didn't need to be afraid. He was in fact restoring the years I had sown in tears. I rejoiced.

The storm was over now.

I finally loved myself enough. I loved myself enough to realize that only a man after God's own heart, my future husband, would be worthy of my virtues. I loved myself enough to listen to God's still small voice when He said, *I love you* and know that I know that I know that He not only meant it but He showed me everyday without fail.

I jumped up and down cheering at the top of my lungs. "Hallelujah, hallelujah. Christ reigns. His love abounds forever and ever. Holy, Holy, Holy, my heart is full of His glory."

After all, this was cause to celebrate. I had taken back what the devil stole from me and found the lover of my soul.

He will wipe away all the tears from their eyes, and there shall be no more death, no sorrow, nor crying, nor pain. All of that has gone forever. Revelation 21:4

When It's All Said And Done

For we know that all things work together for the good of those who love Him and are called according to His purpose.

Romans 8:28

Every time I look back over my life, I get caught up because I can see the places from where God brought me. Just a quick glance over my shoulder and my spirit erupts in praise. I get caught up because you have no idea what my praise cost me.

For me, praise is an acronym. The P stands for purposeful passion, persistence, potential and promise. The R stands for rising above the obstacles of my past that kept me bound with resilience. The A stands for achieving all my life's dreams with an abundant attitude. The I stands for identifying those hindrances from a life full of blessings and peace. The S stands for allowing strength and self-esteem to set the example for others and myself. The E stands for expecting favor with enthusiasm and experiencing life through eyes of faith. PRAISE stands for the God within me propelling me forward.

Understanding my praise is about more than my relationship with Christ. My praise is also about realizing that I am good enough and that I do deserve to live a life of abundance. My praise is for self-love, self-confidence and self-worth. My praise is the realization that I deserve more than what I have settled for in my past. My praise is about loving who I see when I look in a mirror. My praise is the smile that shows the deep dimples that I was born with, which make my eyes dance. My praise is about being confident in my abilities to use the gifts that God gave me to advance His Kingdom. I have been given the gift to motivate and inspire others. I thank God for my praise.

My praise is a powerful weapon. My praise is for every child that has been told that they will never amount to anything. My praise is for every child whose innocence has been stolen. My praise is for that woman living in an abusive relationship. My praise is for the teenager who desires to go to college but doesn't have the vision and foresight to believe that anything is possible. My praise is for a woman in a relationship that yields no fruit because she doesn't believe that she deserves more. My praise is for the broken and contrite spirit who wants to take their life. My praise is a hope and a promise that the best is yet to come. My praise is for people with a big audacious dream in their bosom.

My praise is about abundance. Abundance is not material; it is living above strife, stress, and contention. My praise knows that God has your back and in all things He guides you and leads you to the path that you should take.

Sometimes I praise the Lord openly, while other times my praise is just between God and me. I am so in love with Jesus. I am finally happy. It feels so good to even say that to you. And to mean it is even more amazing. In fact, it is incredible. I get excited just thinking about how He took ordinary me and gave me an incredible praise.

My praise is because of the experiences, trials, tribulations, innocent fun and dreadful heart aches that I have endured. My praise is confidence and a healthy self-esteem. It is an understanding that simply because He is I am.

When you allow Christ in and give Him free reign, I promise you, your latter will be greater than the rest. You will become incredible. You will realize like I did that the incredible you has been there all along but for the first time, you can clearly identify yourself.

I can't help but praise Him because of my past. God's love is incredible and He used that incredible love to save me! I have finally found a completeness that keeps me smiling no matter what comes my way. I found agape love, the true love that I Corinthians 13: 7 says bears all things, believes all things, hopes all things, endures all things and never fails. When you love yourself because God first loved you, you will never fail.

From the moment I began to conceptualize who I was, I knew I was different. Not better, just different. God did place a special anointing on my life. In God's Word, I learned that many are called but the chosen are few. I am one of the chosen. I know that to whom much is given, much is required and that is why I needed to shed my fears and write my story. I had to become transparent so that someone reading this book might be blessed.

I really couldn't hold onto the things from my past. If I wanted God to truly work in me, and if I wanted God to love me the way that I desired to be loved, I really needed to let things go and allow him to change and mold me. I had to let go of the heartaches that I suffered at the hands of my family. The broken dreams and promises that I gave to myself had to go. It wasn't easy. It required me to get to a place where I could quiet my flesh to really deal with the things that I wanted God to change in me. To get here, there was much praying and fasting! But doing that had its rewards. I put myself in the position of becoming happy, finding peace and joy in my spirit. I found a place where I realized that I was a great person.

I needed to stop allowing myself to be bound to those things that told me that I was not good enough and that I didn't deserve the best out of life. I allowed my past to be the reason why I did the things I did. I was always playing the blame game but God said not so. He said that I needed to make changes so that people could see His love in me.

If God can change me, He can change anybody. You just have to be a willing vessel and take a hard look at yourself so that He can take control and make you His masterpiece.

My parents both lent great characteristics of themselves to make me who I am. Today I know that when they came together, they made something incredible.

My mother and I have an incredible relationship today. Once I graduated from college, she moved back to Delaware and we started to get to know each other. We talk everyday and I feel that she truly is a dear friend. I can share anything with her and she supports me in all that she can. Once she got out of prison, she made some significant changes in her life, stayed clean and focused on building a better life. My mother is incredible.

My dad is a big supporter of my endeavors as well. I have a tremendous amount of respect for him. He held it down when we needed him. I thank my father for my love of knowledge. I know that he is proud of me. He finally learned how to show me that he loved me and our relationship rejoiced as a result of his openness. I now get excited to talk with him. Although he struggles with his past, I feel confident that he will soon realize that he, too, is incredible.

My stepmother and I have come a long way. I grew up, got rid of the anger and learned to accept her for who she is. She has realized her mistakes and I have forgiven her. Incredible things are coming her way.

It I had it to do all over again, I would have done so many things differently. But my life has been done the way it was supposed to be done so that on the day that you are reading this book you realize that because of my past, you deserve more. More is your God-given right and privilege in life. No matter what you have in your life right now, if you are not happy, you deserve more. You deserve abundance. You deserve to be happy. You deserve a love that bears all things, endures all things and hopes all things. You deserve to look in the mirror and love what you see.

For so long, I wasn't sure who I really was. I was so used to putting on airs and pretending that I was grand and wonderful. In my mind, no one could ever know the truth about me because if they knew, no one would like me or want to be with me and my biggest fear would be realized; I would be alone. As I grew stronger in the Lord and got to know myself in the process, I realized that I was a great person. I realized that I was capable of loving and being loved in return. I realized that I had a lot to offer to the lives of others.

I finally allowed the Lord to remove the chip on my shoulder and when I did, the floodgates opened and blessings poured into my life. What I enjoy today is better than the material satisfaction of my past. I have a life more abundant. I believe that the best things in life are free and I live above stress, strife and contention. I have a joy that radiates from my pores and maximizes my passion and enthusiasm to help and edify others. I realized that I deserve more!

I John 1:4 says *we write that your joy may be complete*. I wrote this book with the sincere hope that your praise would be complete.

God's Word in Philippians 1:6 says *being confident of this very thing that he that hath begun a good work in you will perform until the day of Jesus Christ*. Get excited, God is still working on me and He is still working on you.

I pray that my story has inspired you to fervently say, "Because I understand her past, I understand her praise and I am one step closer to finding my own."

Thank you! I pray that God's blessings continue to rest in your bosom. It is my sincere hope that my story has blessed and inspired you.

Be Incredible,

Darnyelle A. Jervey

Author, Speaker, Consultant

Incredible One Enterprises, LLC

www.incredibleoneenterprises.com

www.darnyellespeaks.com

888.801.5794 Office

888.563.5351 Fax

Author of:
If You Understood My Past, You Would Understand My Praise
The Incredible You
Dream the Incredible Journal

3 more Empowering Books coming soon!

See the Invisible, Do the Impossible….so, Dream the Incredible

Book Club Discussion Topics:

I believe that the themes of this book can make awesome discussion topics for a girl's night in, book club, panel discussion, woman's prayer group, etc. Please allow the lessons I learned to provide discussion and wisdom to you and your group. I pray that speaking to the mountains in your life will bring release as they move out of the way and allow you to see clearly and walk into your purpose.

Themes:

Putting confidence in man
Believing that a man is the key to happiness, fulfillment, joy, perfection, etc.
A personal relationship with Christ
The importance of reading God's Word
Self-love
Self-esteem
Molestation
Forgiveness
Settling for less than you deserve
Sound decision making
Premarital sex & unprotected sex
Marriage: What is it? What does it mean?
    Why do we (single people) want it so bad?
Therapy
Lying
Cheating
Listening to hear God's still small voice
The definition of love
Being single
Living a saved life without removing all the fun
Abortion

Fear
Trust
Relationships
Dreams
Sacrificing for the sake of a relationship
Going against your values/morals
Physical abuse
Step-parenting
The affects of drug abuse on children
Incarceration
Being saved and satisfied
Discovering your worth

Need to motivate, inspire, edify or empower your group? You need an Incredible Speaker!

Darnyelle would love to discuss her novels with your book club or fellowship group either in person or via conference call.

Darnyelle would love to inspire, motivate and empower your group or organization. Darnyelle would love to make your next event an Incredible One!

For more information contact:
Incredible One Enterprises, LLC
560 Peoples Plaza #255
Newark, DE 19702
1-888-801-5794
info@incredibleoneenterprises.com
www.incredibleoneenterprises.com
www.darnyellespeaks.com

About the Author

Darnyelle A. Jervey is the founder and Chief Empowerment Officer of Incredible One Enterprises, a full service motivational and empowerment firm headquartered in Newark, Delaware.

Known for her enthusiasm, contagious energy and passionate delivery, Darnyelle will capture your attention and keep it as soon as she opens her mouth! Using music to motivate, empower and inspire, allow Darnyelle to "raise the bar" on your dreams so that you can see the invisible and do the impossible in your life.

Darnyelle, whose name means "**a secret place where dreamers go to dream**," is powerful beyond measure as she builds dreams in the lives of her clients and workshop participants.

She has been inspiring people for years and has gained invaluable experience in sales, network marketing, organizational development, business development, management and human resources. Her professional experience includes 12+ years in various management roles in a Fortune 500 Financial Services Company.

Her resume also includes being a Top Independent Executive Senior Sales Director (promoting 5 women to the ranks of Independent Sales Director) in Mary Kay Cosmetics where she earned 5 Career Cars including 2 Pink Cadillacs and assisted in the home-based business development of 500 independent beauty consultants in 5 years!

A highly energetic and passionate empowerment speaker and consultant, Darnyelle Jervey shares a powerful message that is destined to empower Incredible results and impact change in the lives' of her participants.

Darnyelle's mission is clear: to help you to define the Incredible You. Darnyelle has an **INCREDIBLE** ability to connect with her audience. She is both engaging and entertaining, setting an expectation to challenge her participants to live the **INCREDIBLE** life they were born to live.

She is the author of three books, ***If You Understood My Past, You Would Understand My Praise, Dream the Incredible Journal*** and ***The Incredible You.*** She is currently working on three literary projects.

A professional speaker since 1999, her clients and audiences include Fortune 500 companies, state agencies, small businesses, home-based businesses, faith-based organizations, educational institutions, fraternities and sororities and non-profit organizations. She has received the Black Achiever in Business and Industry Award as well as the Community Commitment Award in her home state of Delaware. She is a member of the New Castle County Chamber of Commerce, Zeta Phi Beta Sorority, Inc, Toast Masters, Intl, MPACT Sisters, Delaware Black Professional Women and the Middletown Area Chamber of Commerce.

She holds Bachelors of Art degree in English from the University of Delaware and is currently pursuing a dual Masters in Business Administration from Goldey-Beacom College.

Darnyelle's philosophy is simple: we all must live an Incredible life filled with P.A.C.E. ™

We must strive to:

Plan with Purposeful Passion

Achieve with an Attitude of Abundance

Create with Consistent Confidence

Execute with Enthusiastic Expectation…..

Have you got the P.A.C.E. ™?
Do you want the P.A.C.E. ™?
How will the P.A.C.E. ™ change your life?

Stay tuned for more great books from Darnyelle A. Jervey that are destined to inspire.

Currently Available:

The Incredible You

Dream the Incredible Journal

Coming Soon:

Back Away From the Incredible SNATCHERS

Marketing the Incredible You

A Christian Fiction Novel: A Quick Work.

Take a sneak peak at A Quick Work:

An Excerpt from A Quick Work

As Peyton settled into her king sized pillow top bed that night, something in her spirit didn't feel right. Even as the plush, satin-sheeted pillows enveloped her petite frame, she felt unsettled. The only place that had always been her haven, suddenly added to the uneasiness that she had been battling all day. It had been a laboriously long day and she'd been lack luster for almost all of it, but this feeling was something more than lack luster. Her heart ached; she took a deep breath and sighed.

It was a slow pain; it crept into the crevices of her soul and then shifted to cause an extreme amount of discomfort. As the pain moved down into her abdomen, there was a vat of nausea resting in the pit of her stomach and she couldn't shake it. She'd eaten three saltines and drank half a can of Ginger Ale to no avail. The feeling wasn't stirring. It was stagnant; causing her to go through the motions of vomiting but with no evidence that she felt sick. Small beads of perspiration began to form on the edge of her temples and trickled down the sides of her milk chocolate colored face.

Her shoulder length hair began to unravel from her once neat chignon at the nape of her neck, which was beginning to tense up at the thought that something was going terribly wrong. She raised her left perfectly arched eyebrow and scoured at the thought that this was all somehow her fault.

Without hesitation, she got up from her bed and knelt on the floor in front of her mahogany wood nightstand. She started to pray but the words were caught in her throat. She exhaled deeply trying to eliminate the remnants of the feeling that was plaguing her soul. Yet it lingered, it meandered, tiptoeing all over her emotions and creating a sensation of regret and disbelief that this was even happening.

When Peyton got up with her knees tight from the strain of shifting all of her weight to her lower body and tears filling in the corners of her honey brown eyes, she did not feel a release. Usually when she took something to the Lord in prayer, she felt better instantly. She was troubled. And she didn't know why; but, she knew for certain it had something to do with *him.* He had been sitting on her stomach causing each episode of her nauseating experience.

Peyton took a look around her bedroom and shook her head. Everything was in its place. She searched for a reason to get up and clean as that always made her feel better. *Where was he*? Her silent inquisition started again. *He should have been home by now.* Instinctively, she reached for her phone and dialed his number again without even looking down at the keypad. The call went straight to voicemail. Without hesitation, she called his home phone number and four lengthy rings later, she again found herself hearing his outgoing voicemail message: "I'm not home right now, you know what to do. Do it at the beep."

Peyton didn't know what to do, that is why she had been praying and fasting all week. It wasn't like Micah to turn his cell phone off. It wasn't like him to disappear. Yeah, they'd had a fight. It was a big fight, the biggest fight they'd ever had, but he was acting out of character even for the magnitude of their argument. Yeah, she'd said some things and he'd said some things, but they'd never gone a whole week without speaking. And this week of all weeks was critical; communication was the key. But the door was locked, Peyton had not been able to get in at all. *Where is he?* She asked herself inwardly again. A deep breath steadied her growing anxiety as she got up from her bed.

As she prepared to take her first sip, the phone rang.

"Finally," she said as she leaned over to grab the phone from its base.

"Hello," she answered.

"Yes, hello, may I speak with Peyton Morgan?" The cold and definitively masculine voice with a slightly southern accent responded.

"May I ask who is speaking?" Peyton checked the clock on her over-the-counter microwave oven; it was two am. Her heart nose-dived a little when she realized that it wasn't Micah.

"Yes, this is Officer Daniels at the Newark Police Department."

"This is Peyton, is everything all right?" She felt her heart beat speed up a little when he introduced himself.

Suddenly, there was static in the phone line and the line went dead.

"Hello, Hello?" Peyton said in a panic stricken tone. *What the devil*? She thought to herself as she attempted to dial the number back.

When she tried the number on her caller id, it said that the number she was trying to reach was a non-working number and that she should try her call again.

"What?" She said, exasperated as she returned the phone to the receiver.

What did the police want with her? Who were they calling regarding? As she continued her personal inquisition, the phone rang again.

"Hello," she answered without even allowing the phone to ring a full time.

"Yes, I'm sorry Ms. Morgan it is Officer Daniels again. The call got disconnected. Because I am not calling from the station, the dispatcher somehow lost the connection. Please accept my apologies." There was a slight hint of warmth in his voice.

"That's okay. What's this about?"

"M'aam, I am out on Elkton Road just southwest of the University of Delaware. Are you familiar with the area? I'm on the corner of Casho Mill Road and Elkton just past the one lane underpass."

"Yes, what's going on, Officer?" Peyton was growing impatient.

"Ms. Morgan, I am sorry to have to be the one to tell you this, but there's been an accident. Your name and number was on the passenger seat of the car."

From Past to Praise

If you loved Darnyelle's Memoir, you must have the companion CD! Listen as Darnyelle shares her INCREDIBLE story of courage, faith, determination and perseverance! Get inspired as she shares 10 keys to make your own personal journey

From Past to Praise.

www.ingramcontent.com/pod-product-compliance
Lightning Source LLC
LaVergne TN
LVHW050624100826
845148LV00011B/1715

9780982028001